The Palmetto

and Its South Carolina Home

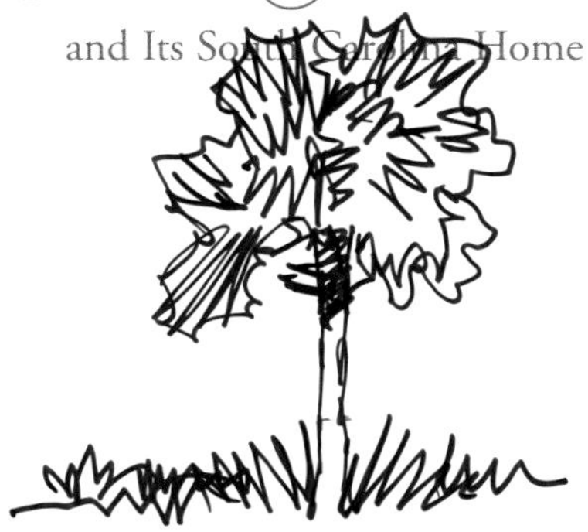

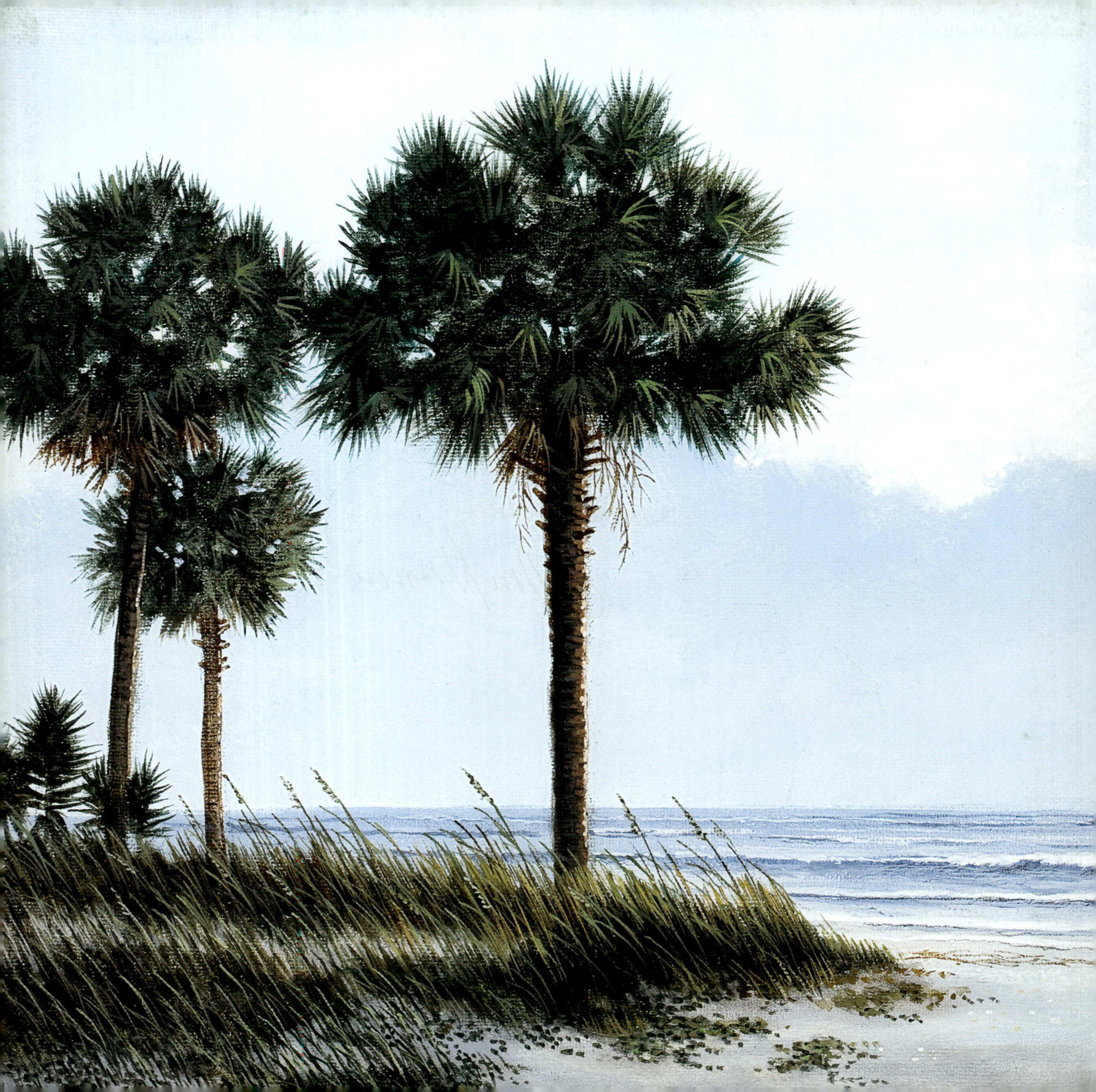

The Palmetto

and Its South Carolina Home

Jim Harrison

The University of South Carolina Press

Published by the University of South Carolina Press
Columbia, South Carolina 29208

www.sc.edu/uscpress

Manufactured in Korea

21 20 19 18 17 16 15 14 13 12 9 8 7 6 5 4 3 2 1

Library of Congress Cataloging-in-Publication Data

Harrison, Jim, 1936–
The palmetto and its South Carolina home / Jim Harrison.
p. cm.
ISBN 978-1-61117-049-8 (cloth : alk. paper)
1. Harrison, Jim, 1936– —Themes, motives. 2. Cabbage palmetto in art.
3. South Carolina—In art. I. Title.
ND237.H335A4 2011
759.13—DC23 2011031530

Frontis: detail from *The Palmettos*

A special thank you to Margaret and Deidre, who patiently prodded, pushed, pulled, and helped get this book over the finish line

Contents

List of Illustrations
viii

About the Artist
Deidre Martin
xi

The Palmetto: An Essay
xix

The Paintings
1

South Carolina's Fascination
with the Palmetto Tree
57

Illustrations

Figures

Photograph of Jim Harrison *xii*

Palmetto Tree Commission Letter *xiii*

Photograph of Gov. John C. West and Jim Harrison *xiv*

Governor's Order of the Palmetto Letter *xv*

Photograph of Gov. Mark Sanford and Jim Harrison *xvi*

The State Flag of South Carolina *58*

The Great Seal of South Carolina *59*

The South Carolina Quarter *59*

The University of South Carolina Logo *60*

Plates

Three Palmettos in the Sand *5*

Big Palmetto *7*

Palmettos in Marsh *9*

Beach and Palmettos *11*

Dark Day on the Marsh *13*

Stormy Palmetto *15*

Palmetto Sunrise *17*

Marsh *18–19*

Marsh Creek *21*
Palmetto and Sunrise *23*
Orange and Brown Sunset *25*
Palmetto Sunset *27*
Palmetto Trees *29*
Palmettos *31*
Palmettos and Marsh *33*
Storm Clouds over Marsh *34–35*
Palmettos in the Morning *37*
The Palmettos *39*
Palmettos in the Sand *41*
Palmettos in Dunes *43*
Dunes and Palmettos *45*
Sky and Palmetto *47*
Three Palmettos *49*
Palmetto Christmas 2007 *50*
Palmetto Christmas 2008 *51*
Palmetto Christmas 2009 *53*
Palmetto Barn *55*

About the Artist

JIM HARRISON LOVES SOUTH CAROLINA and rural America. With a passion for preserving a part of our country that is beginning to slip away far too quickly, he evokes a true appreciation for the old and forgotten. He sees beauty at every turn. His paintings of landscapes and seascapes, old buildings and barns, allow Harrison, in his tranquil way, to place you in his work . . . therefore placing you in his life. He can make you enjoy the skies that you haven't slowed down enough to notice and the land and sea you didn't take the time to appreciate. Harrison's work reflects on times past . . . what once was, what should have been, and what we long for again.

Jim Harrison was born in his grandmother's house in Leslie, Georgia, in January 1936. When Jim was six years old, his father had a job with the American Telephone and Telegraph Company, and his mother worked as a Southern Bell switchboard operator in Denmark, South Carolina. The Harrisons worked hard to raise and educate Jim and his younger brothers, Phil and Wendel.

Harrison was very involved in the activities of Denmark High School. As the "class artist," he was kept busy on the annual staff, school newspaper, and class bulletin boards. His first love was athletics, in which he excelled and was named all state in basketball. He held the South Carolina high school state record for scoring seventy-one points in one basketball game.

During high school summer vacations, Harrison worked as an assistant to a seventy-year-old sign painter, J. J. Cornforth. The elder gentleman taught the aspiring artist how to letter, and for several summers the two traveled the rural areas around Denmark, painting Coca-Cola bulletins on the sides of barns and country stores.

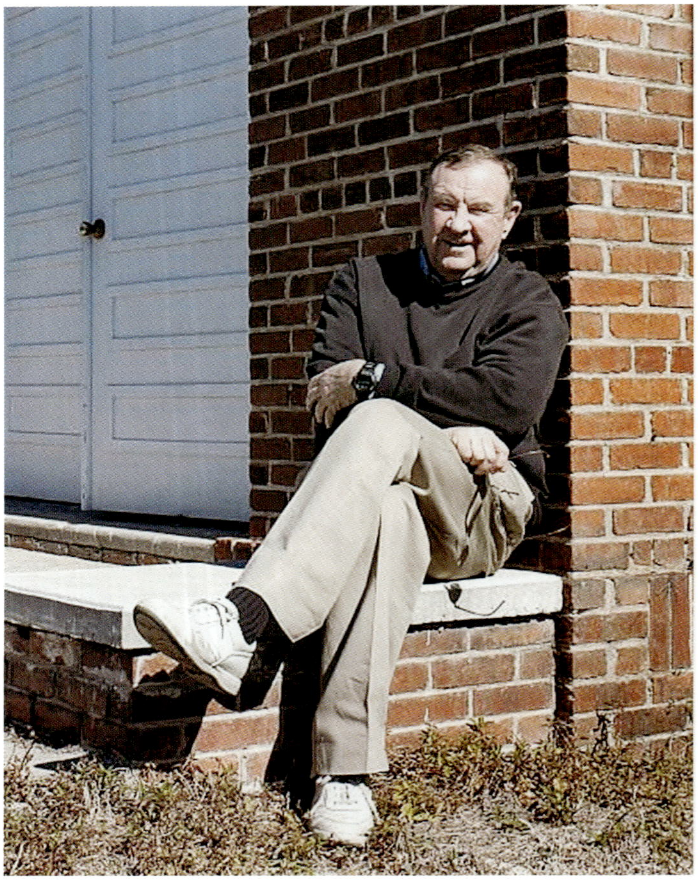

Jim Harrison on brick steps

After high school graduation, Harrison entered the University of South Carolina. Torn between his love of art and the enjoyment of athletics, he pursued a dual major in art and physical education. In 1960 he embarked on a successful eleven-year high school coaching career, and he also scouted for the national league baseball Cleveland Indians from 1965 through 1970. Employed at three schools during that time, he coached football, girls' basketball, and baseball, and he completed his career as a head coach with an overall winning record. But when the time came to choose, his passion for creating memorable works of art and preserving rural America was the stronger influence. In 1970 he declined an offer to join the Furman University football coaching staff and returned to his hometown of Denmark, South Carolina, to pursue art as a career.

In 1972 Harrison had no knowledge of the art market, but he traveled with enthusiasm to New York City for the Fall Greenwich Village sidewalk art show. His only sale during the three-week show was an eighty-five-dollar original, and the trip cost him eight hundred dollars in expenses. Several years on the sidewalk circuit served him well as he learned his trade and the business of art. After several years he had ten galleries selling his originals. He published his first limited edition print, "Coastal Dunes," in 1973, and with it he gained the attention of the nation's leading publisher of limited edition art prints, Frame House Gallery of Louisville, Kentucky. In 1975 Frame House released its first Jim Harrison print, "Rural Americana," and

State of South Carolina

JOHN C. WEST
GOVERNOR

OFFICE OF THE GOVERNOR
COLUMBIA 29211

April 3, 1974

Mr. Jim Harrison
Denmark
South Carolina

Dear Mr. Harrison:

I commission you to paint the Palmetto Tree for the State of South Carolina. It is understood that the original painting will be given to the State of South Carolina to hang in some appropriate place.

Best regards.

Sincerely,

John C. West

JCW/bb

Palmetto Tree Commission Letter

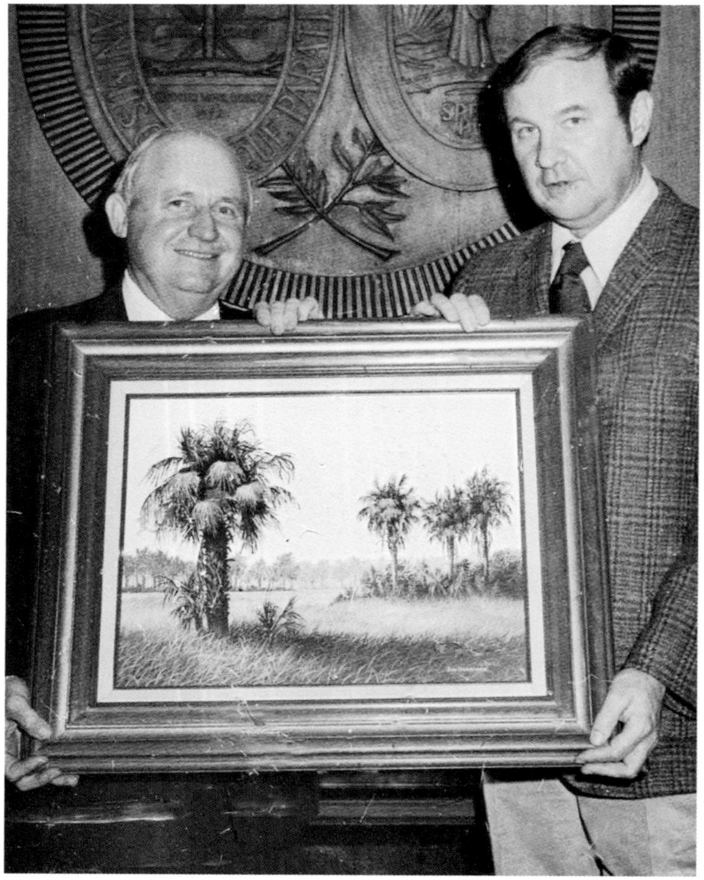

Gov. John C. West and Jim Harrison

that print propelled Harrison on the national scene through the publisher's network of six hundred dealers. He became the undisputed nation's leader in rural Americana art, and many of his prints have appreciated in value up to 3,000 percent of their original cost.

In 1974 Gov. John C. West commissioned Harrison to paint for the State of South Carolina the official painting of the palmetto tree. The painting is now owned by the state and is displayed within the government buildings.

Harrison's success is evidenced by his more than forty years as a full-time artist. Turning his back on the more familiar path—a career in high school and college athletics—he embraced his dream to become an artist. With talent, hard work, and perseverance, he has sold out more than one hundred limited editions of prints made from his paintings, and there are now thousands of collectors of his work across the country. Harrison's works are featured in personal and corporate art collections across the country including the Coca-Cola Company in Atlanta, Georgia; the Maytag Corporation in Newton, Iowa; the Philip Morris Company in New York, New York; the Leo Burnett Company in Chicago, Illinois; and the Augusta National Golf Club in Augusta, Georgia.

Harrison has also had successful one-man shows at the prestigious Hammer Galleries in New York City and the Conacher Gallery in San Francisco. His paintings

State of South Carolina

Office of the Governor

MARK SANFORD
GOVERNOR

POST OFFICE BOX 12267
COLUMBIA 29211

September 21, 2008

Mr. James Wiley Harrison
175 Hammond Street
Denmark, South Carolina 29042

Dear Jim,

On behalf of the people of South Carolina, I am pleased to award you the Order of the Palmetto – our state's highest civilian honor for service. This award is in recognition of all you have done to better our part of the world over the years.

A life well spent is a life that includes others. How prophetic that a summer job painting Coca-Cola bulletins on the sides of barns and country stores would propel you into the hearts and souls of folks here in South Carolina and literally across the globe through your love of preserving our past with a paintbrush. Your paintings of palmetto trees, covered bridges, vast expanses of water, sunsets and other rural and local lore are as much a part of the culture of our land as Mom and apple pie, and folks are reminded of kinder, gentler times by simply looking at one of your paintings hanging on their walls or receiving a Christmas card from a friend depicting a rural store and home covered with snow. For many, these images are a nostalgic walk down memory lane and for others, a sense of life less hectic.

In addition, you have given generously of your time and talents as an ambassador for many causes, and I am impressed just looking at the breadth of your devotion to others, including your contributions to South Carolina 4-H Clubs, the USC Alumni Center, the Boards of Voorhees and Denmark Technical Colleges, the Denmark Downtown Development Association, USC Aiken, SCETV, the Agricultural Heritage Center, the South Carolina National Heritage Corridor Partnership Board, as a little league coach, as a Sunday School teacher – and the list goes on. These any many other worthwhile endeavors have greatly benefited from your leadership, wisdom, encouragement and strong support.

In closing, I paraphrase several of your quotes, "Keep standing in front of the wrecking ball with your paintbrush and pen … and continue your love affair with old buildings, old things, and old ways." For your work in preserving our heritage on canvas and in our hearts, we extend our gratitude. You are, indeed, a legend in your own time, and your influence in the world of art will be as enduring as your art itself. While it is difficult to compress and describe all you have done for your community and our state in a letter, your generosity and talent will have a positive effect on our citizens for generations to come. Thank you for upholding the highest ideals of servant leadership in everything that you do.

Sincerely,

Mark Sanford

MS/jbn

Order of the Palmetto Letter

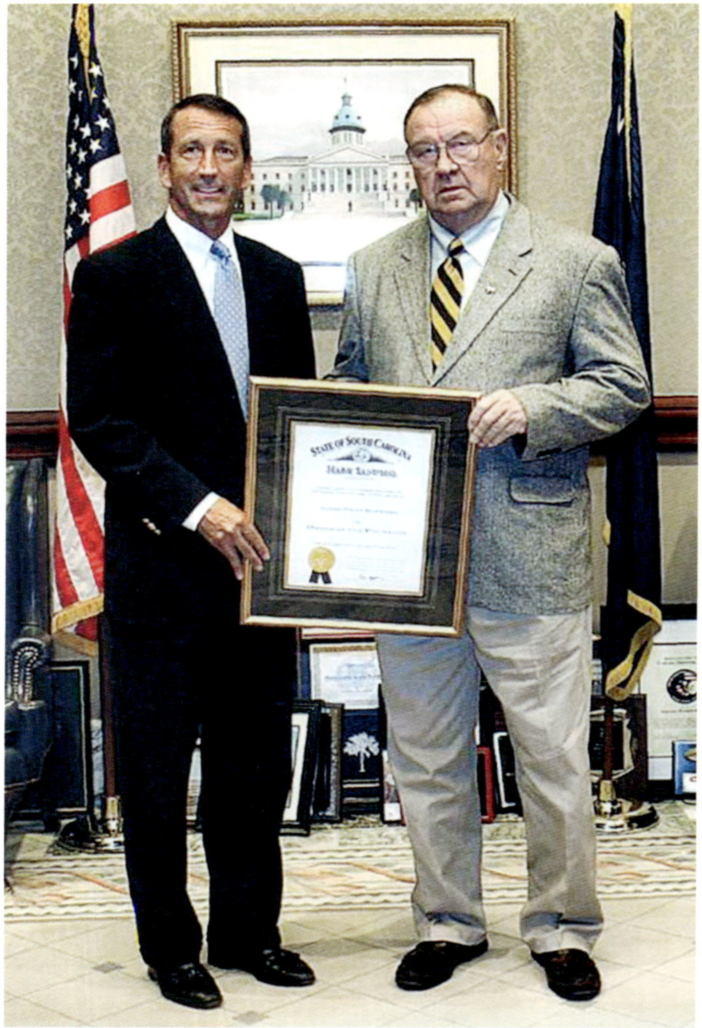

Gov. Mark Sanford and Jim Harrison

have been included in the annual shows at the highly regarded National Academy Gallery in New York.

In addition Harrison has received such recognition as being named to the Honorable Order of Kentucky Colonels by the governor of Kentucky, having a park in Denmark named in his honor, and being named a distinguished adjunct professor at the University of South Carolina Aiken. He has served on the boards of South Carolina National Bank, the Security Federal Bank, Vorhees College, Denmark Technical College, and the Denmark Downtown Development Association. Also, being a strong advocate for the mentally ill, he served on the board of the governor's legislative council for mental health and mental retardation at an earlier time in his life and worked tirelessly in that effort. In 2008 he was honored by Gov. Mark Sanford of South Carolina with the prestigious Order of the Palmetto Award for his many years of service as a citizen of our state. In May 2010 Jim Harrison was awarded an honorary doctorate of fine arts by President Harris Pastides of the University of South Carolina in recognition of Harrison's many successful years as a professional artist, the prestige he has brought to the university and the state, and his generosity to a wide range of charitable organizations.

Harrison has been a licensee of the Coca-Cola Company for more than ten years and produces the Coca-Cola Calendar for collectors each year. This relationship is a visible demonstration of his love of the well-known trademark, which he first painted on the side of Brooker's Hardware Store when he was fourteen years old and apprenticed of to J. J. Cornforth.

IN ADDITION TO CRAFTING HIS ARTWORK, Harrison is the author or co-author/artist of several books, including *Pathway to a Southern Coast, Country Stores, American Christmas, The Passing, Jim Harrison: His World Remembered,* and *The Jim Harrison Cookbook: Southern Cooking and Southern Stories.*

DEIDRE MARTIN

The Palmetto

An Essay

FOR THOUSANDS OF YEARS the stubborn South Carolina palmetto tree has welcomed each new sunrise ready to stand steadfast against the constant changing environment of the coastal region. The revered Carolina lowcountry area where the salt water meets the land is the natural home of the Sabal palmetto. Surviving in one of the harshest environments, the state's icon often endures hot 100-degree summer days and occasional subfreezing nights of winter.

With a South Carolina arrogance of "bring it on," the tree combats the testing forces of hurricane winds and surging surfs. It gracefully bends but seldom breaks, representing well our symbol of strength, determination, and survival.

All living things are influenced by the environment where they live and so it is with the palmetto and its coastal home. The South Carolina coast by definition is a strip of land about twelve miles wide that is parallel to the shoreline. This 150,000-acre maritime environment was flooded and expanded by the melting ice ten thousand years ago, and it is much more complex and important than can be detailed here. Protected by 35 barrier islands, the massive estuary complex influences life systems far beyond the Carolina shore.

We South Carolinians dearly love our tree, and even more so we worship the coastal land that it calls home. It was in the ocean that all life was born billions of years ago, and from that underwater world the first tetrapod crawled out of the surf, clung hold to a bit of land, and pulled itself on shore to begin the long process of evolution.

Life on the land portion of the earth has now fully developed, but it is still very much dependant on the ocean that surrounds us. South Carolinians have a very strong ongoing relationship with the salty waters, and for whatever reasons inlanders are drawn to the coastal regions of the state.

Over and over again we return to the water's edge. There, while under scorching summer suns or while gazing at the wonderment of moonbeams dancing across gentle waves, we pay our regular homage to the waters we came from four hundred million years ago. It is baffling and much more than a biological coincidence that all humans have the same percentage of salt in their blood that exists in the ocean water. Perhaps the constant yearning to go back is a yearning to return home to the world of salt water. We are truly children of the sea, and likewise we are eternal kindred visitors to the home of the palmetto.

It is so appropriate that our state tree has found a way to thrive only a stone's throw from the Atlantic surf. To understand, appreciate, and admire the palmetto's toughness and enduring quality, we must be fully aware of its environment and the many daily happenings of the ocean, on the beach, and in the salt marsh areas. Taken as a whole, the coastal landscape appears calm and beautiful, and at first glance one would hardly suspect it capable of delivering such cruel daily poundings and punches. It is no wonder that here is an ultimate testing ground for the durability and endurance of plants and animals.

Survival is the order of every day, and the daily dramas are all part of the fascinating allure of the palmetto's home. A look at that environment should start right at the shoreline of the Mother of All Life, the ocean.

At a distance the huge body of ocean water is a picture of rhythmic tranquility seemingly meant only for visual enjoyment. On a closer look the ocean is one of the most intriguing and awesome powers known to us. With an ageless, untiring strength the greenish-gray water regularly swells and dips as the wind pushes it forward toward the land.

The sloping sandy underwater shoals cause the moving waves to drag bottom, rise, and curl upward before cresting and crashing down, continuing to push the turbulent foaming water toward the beach. Time and time again, hour after hour, day after day, for thousands of centuries, this has occurred regularly with the breakers spraying salt water that throws off cutting shell bits and sand on whatever other vegetation dares to join the palmetto as our first line of defense against the intrusion and erosion.

From the tallest viewpoint on the front line of the erosion battle zone, the palmetto stands over and watches the scurry of activities below on the beach. The lateral area between the low tide mark and the high tide mark supports no vegetation as it is rigorously washed constantly by the flooding and ebbing of the tides.

The created hay line at the upper mark is the spawning ground for some short grasses and vegetation, but the stalwart of the ground cover is the sea oat. A companion defender against erosion, the chest-high wild relative of the cultivated grain plants watches the backside of the palmetto as the tree bends inland with the forceful winds. The sea oats also have the ability to bend but do not break. Not only is it a battler; it is also a builder against erosion.

The sea oat and its fighting partner, the panic grass, learned early as small plants to catch blowing sand particles and drop them around themselves. The instinct of colonization and survival runs strong with them, and as mature plants the grasses continue building the sand of the dunes. The advantage of one plant usually comes at the disadvantage of another but not so with the palmetto, whose root system does not compete with other plants.

Front row palmettos do not often propagate themselves, and so the younger trees get their start some distance from the encroaching surf. As the water and wind erode away the frontline dunes, the sea oats continue the work of building new dunes a few feet inland. The undermining surf constantly attacks the lower levels of the palmetto root system and washes away support. The process causes the tree to tilt forward, and with time it can find itself leaning and standing alone inside the high tide line.

Bravely it persists, yet the power of the surf and force of the massive sea behind it wins the battle, and the tree eventually floats away. The good news is that as one tree on the beach front gives way to the elements just behind the front line, hundreds more have self-propagated and stand ready for the task of the erosion battle. It is sometimes difficult to determine if the sea is moving toward the marsh or the marsh is moving toward the sea. Some of the sand from the erosion process on the beach is washed in and around to the leeward marsh side to support the new dunes.

The soft sound of a breeze rustling the endless field of marsh grass would never give evidence of the millions of things going on beneath the gentle swaying leaves of the Spartina plants. The beauty of the area speaks of serenity and solitude, but scampering around in the shaded marsh mud are thousands of visible creatures and even millions more that are not seen by the naked eye. All living things there are constantly competing and battling for their lives. Much dependence for their survival is placed on the living and dying of the very plants under which they seek cover.

The fast-growing grass provides the overhead protection, but actually few animals feed on the living plants. However, when the grass dies and bacteria begin the decomposition process, the rotted particles provide food for many smaller organisms. These smaller animals in turn provide food for the birds and fish and so on up the food chain. The grass is very important to the entire food chain, and no other crop in the plant kingdom contributes as much nourishment to such a variety of creatures.

Out in this broad field of grass, the palmetto tree does make its presence known on the small isolated hammock islands that dot the tidal wetlands. It is on these isolated spots that some larger wildlife find refuge and food from the stalwart palmetto. Birds, deer, small mammals, and reptiles make their home here.

An occasional palmetto dares to stand alone in the middle of the marsh away from firm land, and such is the epitome of courage. Yet those brave ones find it more difficult to survive the force of the wind as it has less support in the wet marsh mud. As nature gives, nature also takes away, and sooner than later so go those solo palmettos. There is no doubt that it was not meant for trees or people to venture out and survive in the middle of the salt marsh.

It is around the edges of the marsh, just beyond the high tide mark, where the palmetto thrives and follows its natural growth patterns. Those trees there in the partial shade of the taller pines and large oaks grow wider crowns and remain shorter.

It is here that we find the palmetto in its best-suited home, and if left unbothered, it profusely self-propagates and enjoys a greater chance of survival. It is in these locations that we find Sabal specimens whose profiles best visually represent our state symbol. The Sabal palmetto is a favorite of the palm tree family. Typical of this unique and complex species is a large robust tree with a single sturdy, unbranching trunk that occasionally may reach heights of ninety feet and a trunk diameter of twenty-four inches. The stately structure has large graceful fan shaped fronds that form a twelve- to eighteen-foot crown. The most northerly and abundant of all the palms, the Sabal's tolerance to high water tables, hot temperatures, and an abundance of salt permits it to thrive on the edges of the salt marshes. The tree matures slowly, but it has no cambium tissue, and therefore no annual growth rings develop. Specimens are known to live up to 75 years.

Unlike other palms the Sabal has no crown shaft, and the smooth leaf stalks emerge directly from a cabbagelike terminal growth bud at the top of the trunk. The fronds spread in all directions, sometimes reaching lengths of nine feet. Forty to sixty smooth leaflets approximately thirty inches long grow from the end of the fronds in a palmate form. The dull matte medium-green-to-yellow leaflets develop tan edges and tips as they grow older. This evergreen is supported by a deep-penetrating root system reaching fifteen feet or more into a variety of soils. The underground stem is short and bulbous, surrounded by a dense mass of contorted roots. From those roots the thinner light-orange roots grow to the maximum distance reaching the necessary dampness needed to survive.

During June and July small fragrant yellowish-white flowers are abundant and are borne in large clustered panicles on drooping branched clusters extending up to eight feet long beyond the leaves. The flowers produce black, shiny fruits about one-half inch in diameter, and each fruit has one seed. Seeds may remain dormant for years and often are transported by water, wind, and the droppings of birds.

Research has shown seeds that often are transported many miles from the original location. Most of the seed germination takes place from the middle to late summer. The seedling growth the first year consists of only a small primary root and one fully expanded leaf.

The slow-growing young plant takes years before a trunk begins to form; when full grown, the trunk is uniform in diameter from the base to the top. As new stalks and leaves emerge from the top terminal growth bud, the older stalks and leaves are shed, and the bases, or boots, of the fronds cling to the trunk all the way to the ground in a crisscross pattern. Some trees may totally shed the leaves, leaving a rough, fibrous brown trunk, and eventually the trunk will age to a smooth gray surface with circular furrows and vertical cracks.

Palmettos first made their way to South Carolina following the Ice Age. As the earth began to warm and the ice covering North America started melting, the plant life changed and deciduous forests began to develop. South Carolina gradually warmed to the temperatures we have today, and at some point in the four to five thousand years of the warming period, the first palmetto tree seeds floated here from Central or South America before germinating in our coastal area. Further distribution resulted from the eaten seeds landing with the droppings from migratory birds traveling to the North from the South.

The first humans to view the palmetto were the descendants of the Asians who came across a land bridge between Asia and North America thousands of years ago. This passageway was 350 feet above water because the freezing glaciers had trapped large amounts of water and caused the water levels of the ocean to fall. When the Ice Age peaked, giant glaciers at least a mile thick covered much of North America and Europe, but ice sheets never developed in South Carolina. The megafauna (that is, the large animals) that thrived and roamed the area were plentiful in our state and attracted nomadic hunters from the Northwest who had migrated here in search of more food.

The Native Americans by that time were far advanced from the first immigrants from Asia, and they began to settle in more specific locations along the seafood-laden coastal regions. Late during this period of our state's history, the Indians began to establish true permanent social communities and their domestic tools and skills were improving.

The abundant palmetto tree served many uses for those first residents of the Carolina lowcountry. The early settlers made their homes among the plentiful palmettos and used them wisely as building materials. The palm trunks were used as poles to support their chickee huts, which were covered with waterproof thatched roofs made from the fronds. Split logs covered their floors. Scrub brushes were crafted from the fibrous materials taken from the trunks and the leaf sheathes, and baskets were woven from sun-dried fronds. The trunks were cut and hollowed out to serve as pipes to transport water. Troughs were made by splitting the trunks and shaving out the middle and then covering them with porous leaf fronds so as to let the fresh rainwater trickle through for storage. There is some evidence that canoes were carved from the tree trunks.

These early people discovered that the inner portion of the tree's terminal bud was edible both raw and boiled and were an excellent food source. The hearts are slender ivory-colored 1- to 1½-inch cylinders about 4 inches long, and the crunchy heart has rings throughout, like onions have. The terminal bud and its surrounding tender leaves when boiled have a cabbage taste. In today's world it has been referred to as "swamp cabbage" and probably is the basis for the name "cabbage palmetto." The heart of palm is now considered "a millionaire's salad" and is served in expensive restaurants; it is known for its extreme tenderness and delicacy.

Those early Indian cooks stone-ground tender young fronds to mix with water and made a salty bread, and from the black fruit, which has a prunelike flavor, they made a sweet bread meal. Bees gathered the tree's pollen, and a tasty palmetto tree honey was produced; molasses was made from the black berries. Salt was gathered from palmetto trunks by first burning them. The seeds and the berries had the medicinal ability to lower fevers and help relieve pain.

With all that said and done, the best was yet to come for the palmetto. It was on June 28, 1776, that the tree shined the strongest and won the hearts of all Americans. It was then, in the heat of summer and during the stress of battle, that the palmetto tree earned a prominent place in American history and a permanent place on the South Carolina state flag and state seal. Years later it was officially designated the state tree.

On that day the many cut palmetto logs that were used to reinforce the walls of Fort Sullivan strongly held their positions and did their jobs well. The hurriedly built American fort was strategically located on the southern tip of Sullivan's Island at the mouth of the Charleston Harbor. All eyes were focused on this tiny spot in South Carolina and the enormous importance of this battle for America's freedom from the tyranny of England.

The little fort's position offered the only defense of Charleston against the nine large English warships headed their way. There some twenty-nine hundred British invaders underestimated the will of the four hundred men of the Second South Carolina Regiment and the might of their small palmetto fort. Packed with marsh mud and beach sand to give support to the palmetto walls, the logs stood ready to thwart the military threat from the sea. Early that morning the silence of the hour erupted into a barrage of the nine ships' three hundred large cannons broadsiding the fort but to no avail. The soft palmetto logs simply absorbed the best the British could throw, and the double ten-foot walls held fast and withstood the shelling.

At some time during the nine-hour battle, the staff holding the blue and white homemade flag received a hit bringing it to the ground outside the fort's front wall.

Young Sgt. William Jasper braved the enemy fire, retrieved the flag, and replanted it atop the fort's wall. His bravery and quick actions inspired the men to even a greater effort and later earned him the gift of the battle sword that had belonged to President John Rutledge of South Carolina.

The determined South Carolinian patriots inside the fort had only thirty-one cannons and very little gunpowder with which to match the stronger British forces. Their leader, Col. William Moultrie, ordered the men to hold their fire until the smoke from the British shelling had cleared and then carefully make their shots count. The skill, the accuracy, and the determination of the Carolina warriors trumped the might of the British forces, and the colonies' move for independence was well on its way. Under the blue flag with its white crescent gorget symbol, South Carolinians and their palmetto defenses had not only defeated and turned away the six remaining battleships, but the patriots did considerable damage to the British confidence and the British pride.

The victory on that small island that long June day not only ensured the safety of the port of Charleston but also brought many people to join the patriots' cause. Gen. George Washington's army had struggled with little success in the North. The strong victory by South Carolinians proved that the South could stand toe-to-toe with the stronger enemy and wage successful war against the Redcoats. With the strength of the palmetto log fort under the South Carolina flag, the first giant step was taken declaring our independence. Less than a week later, on the Fourth of July, the delegates in Philadelphia signed the Declaration of Independence and our nation was born. The palmetto tree had arrived, and this was its finest hour.

Overleaf: detail from *Marsh Creek*

The Paintings

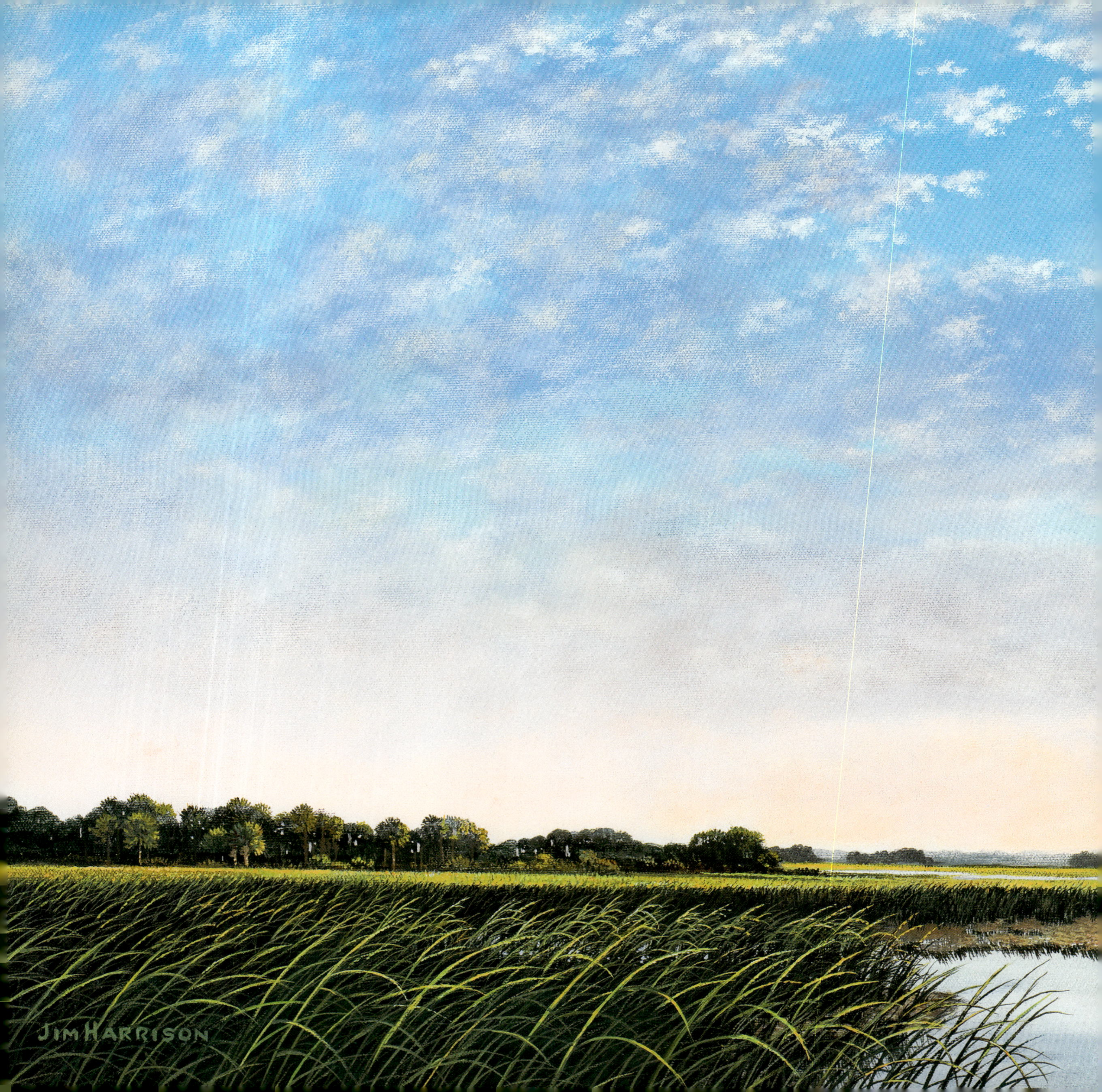
JIM HARRISON

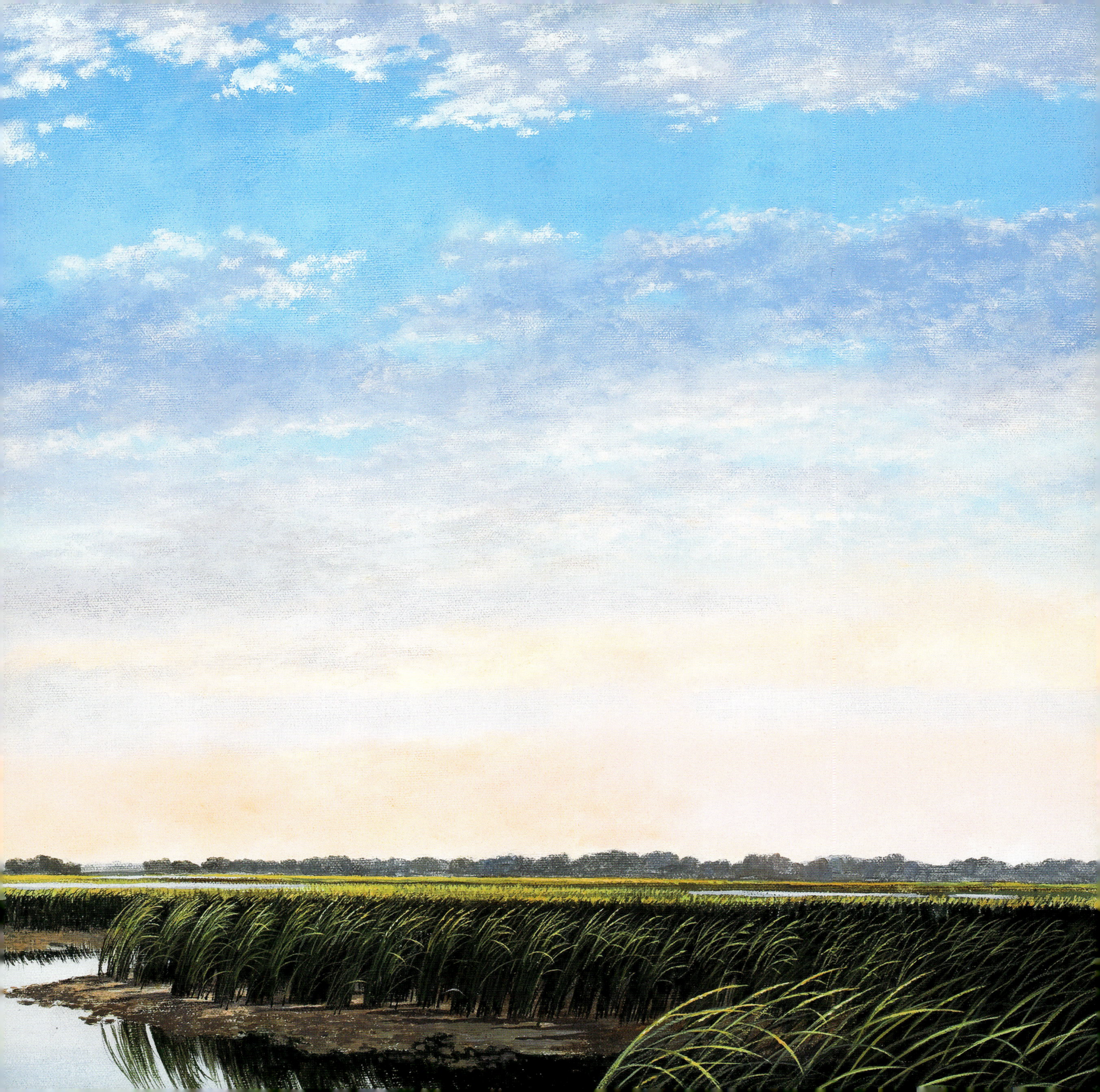

THE SOUTH CAROLINA COAST is quite a special place. My artwork represents my southern heritage with a wide range of images from coastal to rural Americana scenes. Recently I have refocused on capturing the timeless beauty of our state's coastal areas and South Carolina's state tree in particular. The palmetto tree is an image that is very much a part of our state's past, present, and future, and it represents not only the beauty but also the strength of our state and its people.

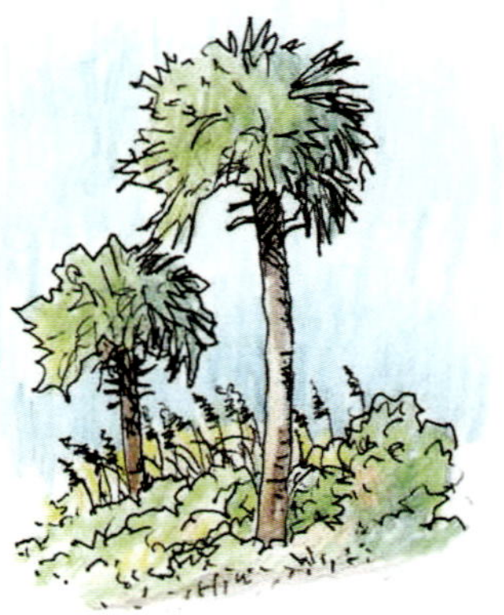

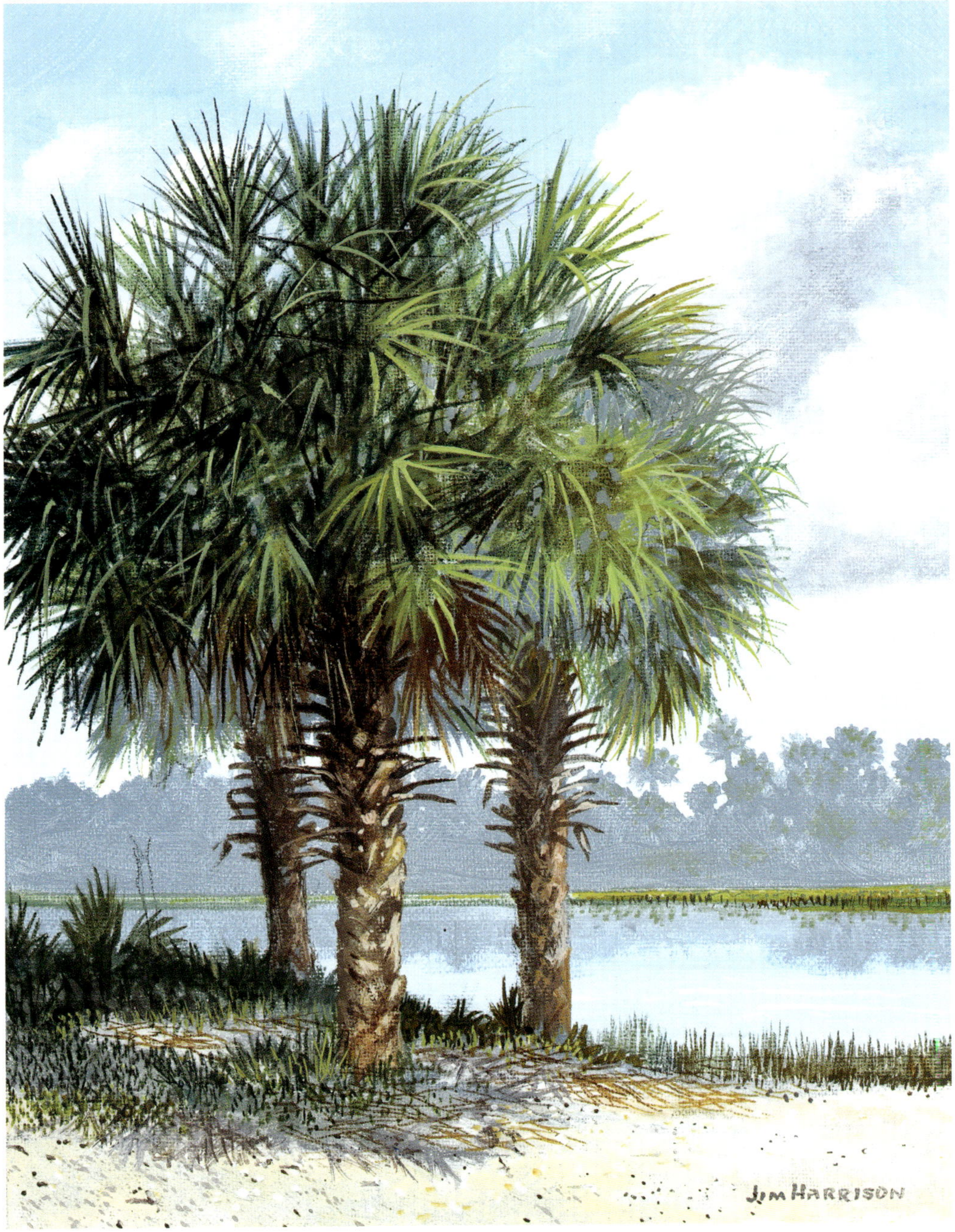

Three Palmettos in the Sand

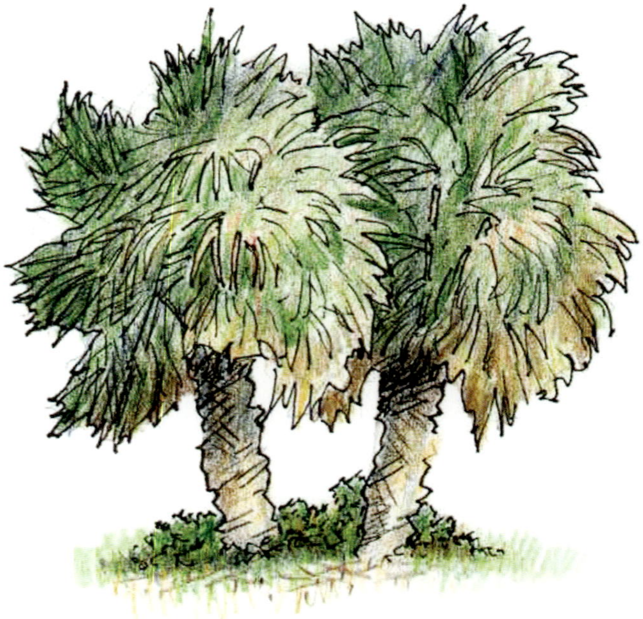

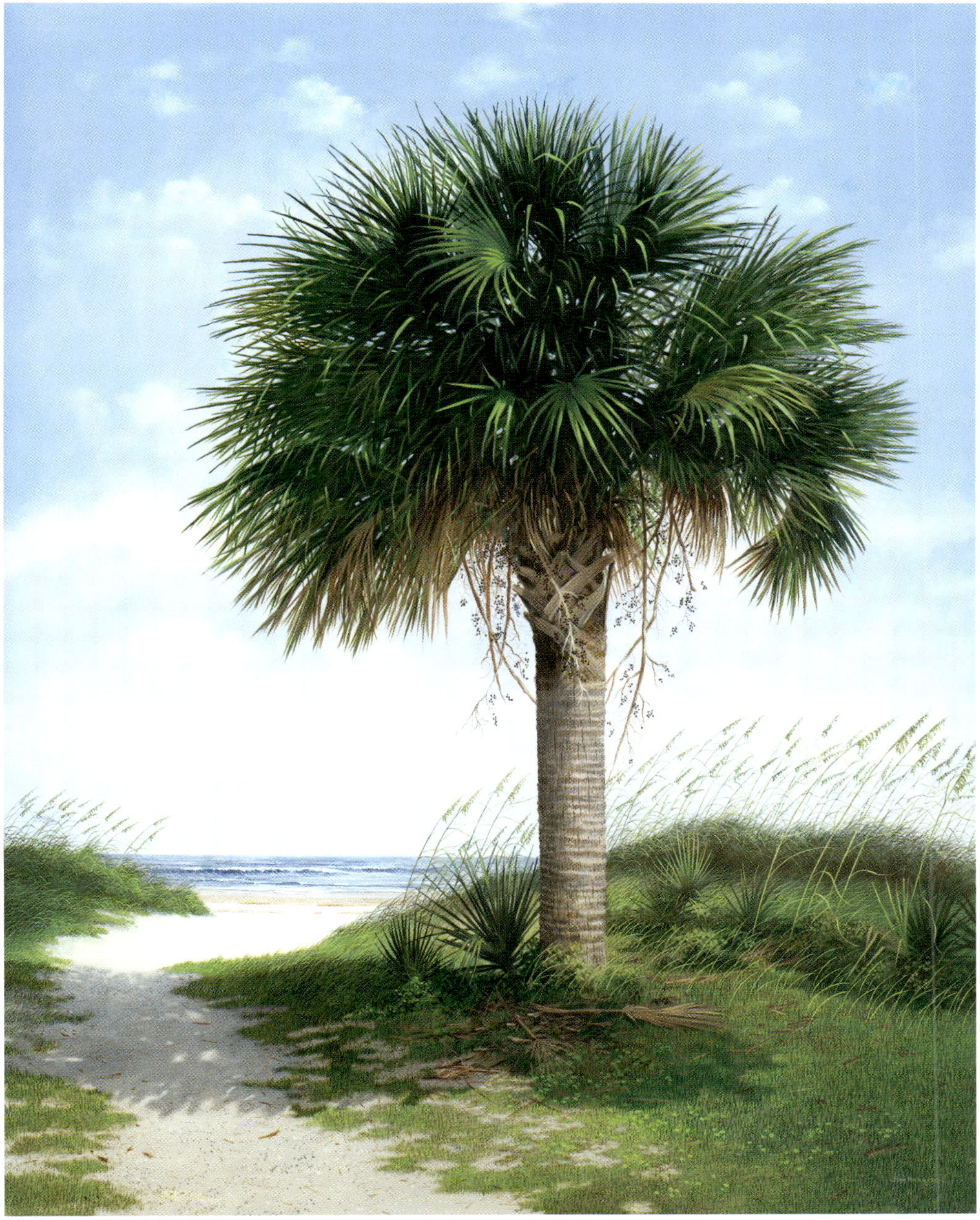

Big Palmetto

WATER PLAYS AN IMPORTANT PART in most people's lives, and we all seem to be drawn to it, whether it is in the form of a pond, a river, a lake, or an ocean. Being a lowcountry resident, I have always been particularly drawn to the marshes and the ocean. Painting these landscapes helps me express the love that I have for South Carolina, and most all of the subjects I paint can be found in the Palmetto State.

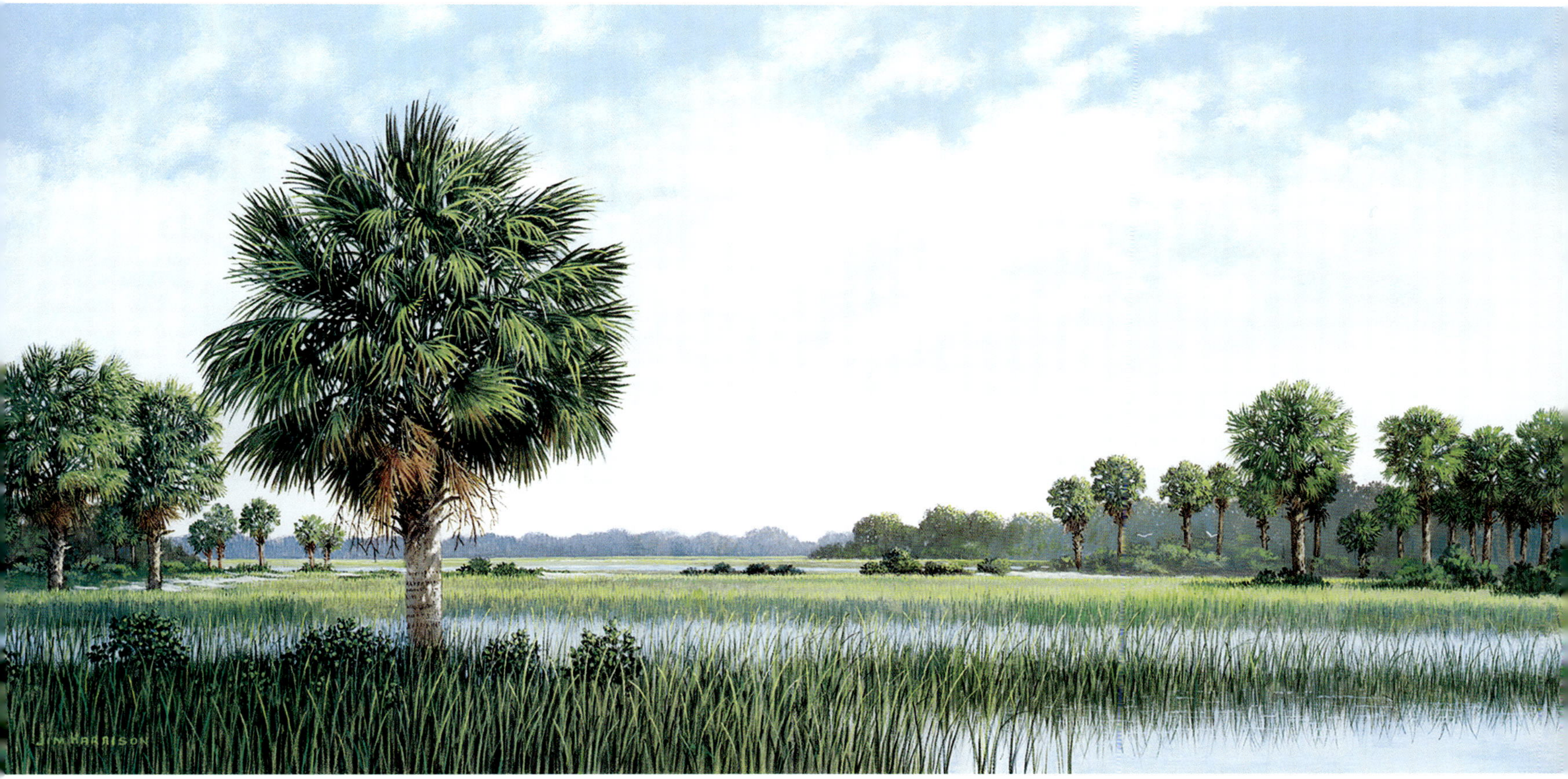

Palmettos in Marsh

THE COASTAL AREA is a magnificent learning ground for artists. Seeing the line of the horizon and the ocean, one becomes aware of the depth and distance that the human eye can see. To paint that distance with the illusion of miles between the foreground of trees and the beach stretching on to the horizon is no easy task. It was in a similar setting that I first began to understand the power of color and linear perspective.

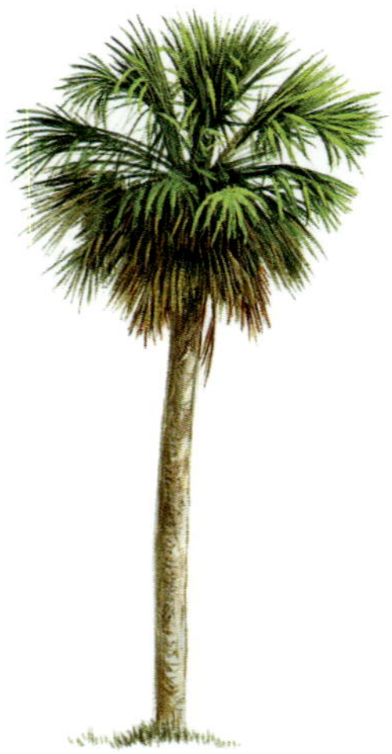

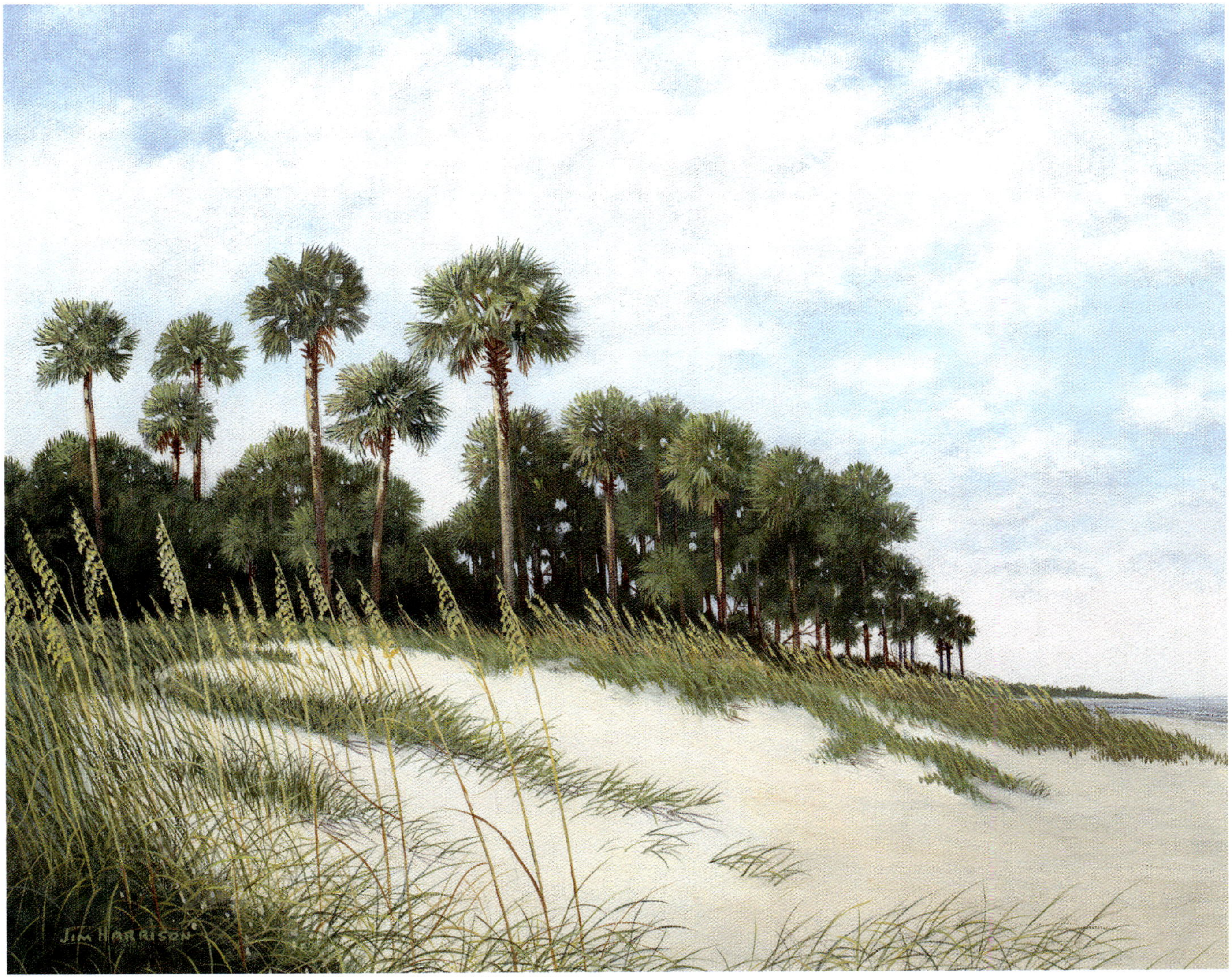

Beach and Palmettos

I WORKED ONE SUMMER COACHING at a camp located right at the edge of the ocean with the marsh at our back. A hundred yards east were the sand dunes, and a hundred yards west was the edge of the salt marsh. There was a maintenance man who had worked nearby all his life, and I was impressed with his ability to predict the weather based on what he saw in the sky. By relying on such simple sayings as "Red sky at night, sailor's delight, but red sky in the morning, a sailor's fair warning," counting the number of times a cricket chirped, or watching the way ants moved, the old gentleman was pretty accurate with his weather predictions. I learned new ways to look at those ever-changing skies.

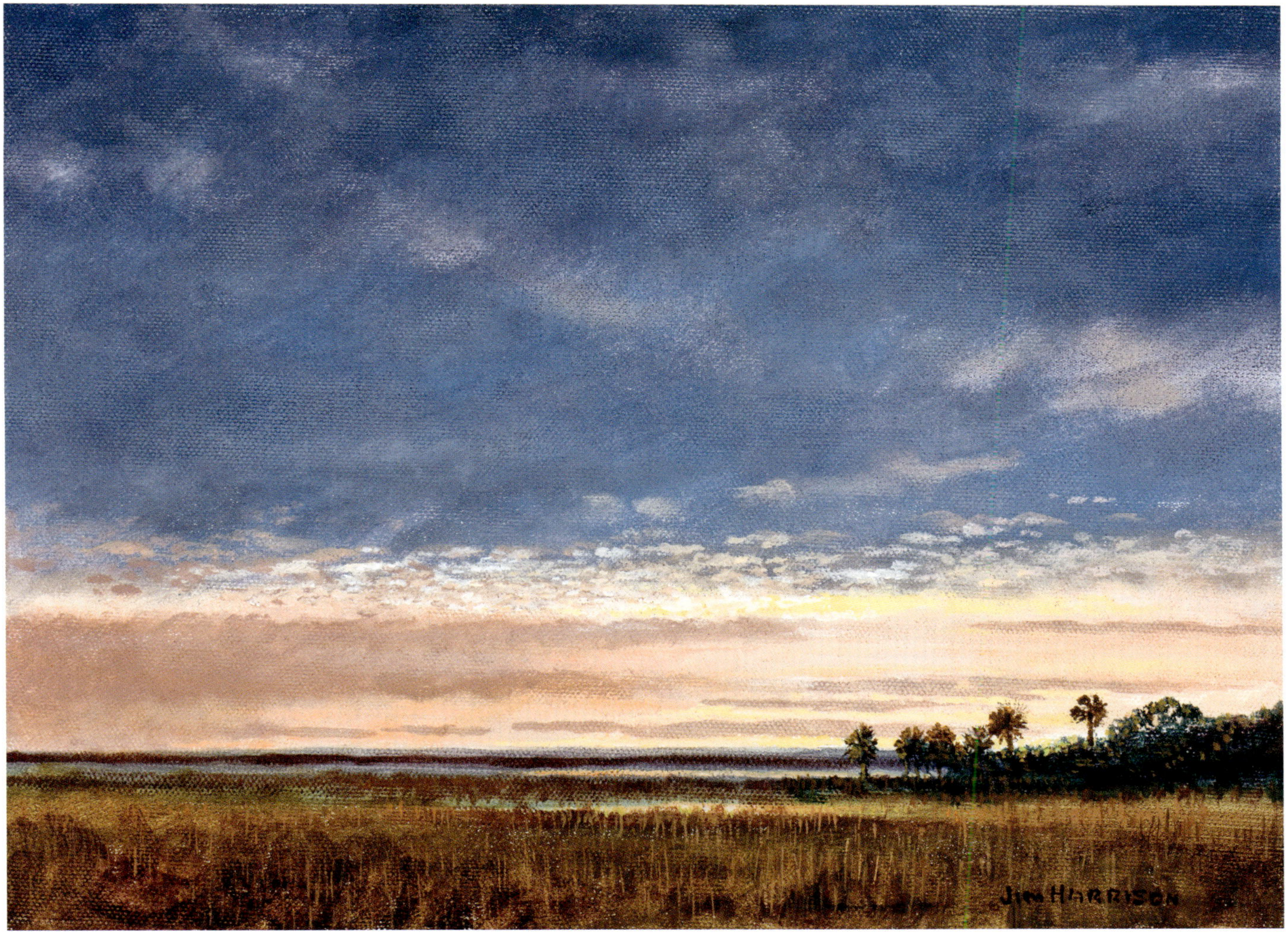

Dark Day on the Marsh

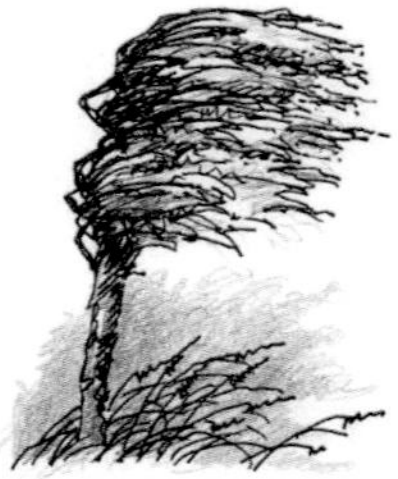

A STORM BREWING over the marsh is a pretty magnificent, yet daunting, thing to witness. The colorful sky, the rough water, and the powerful wind remind us that we are not in control of nature.

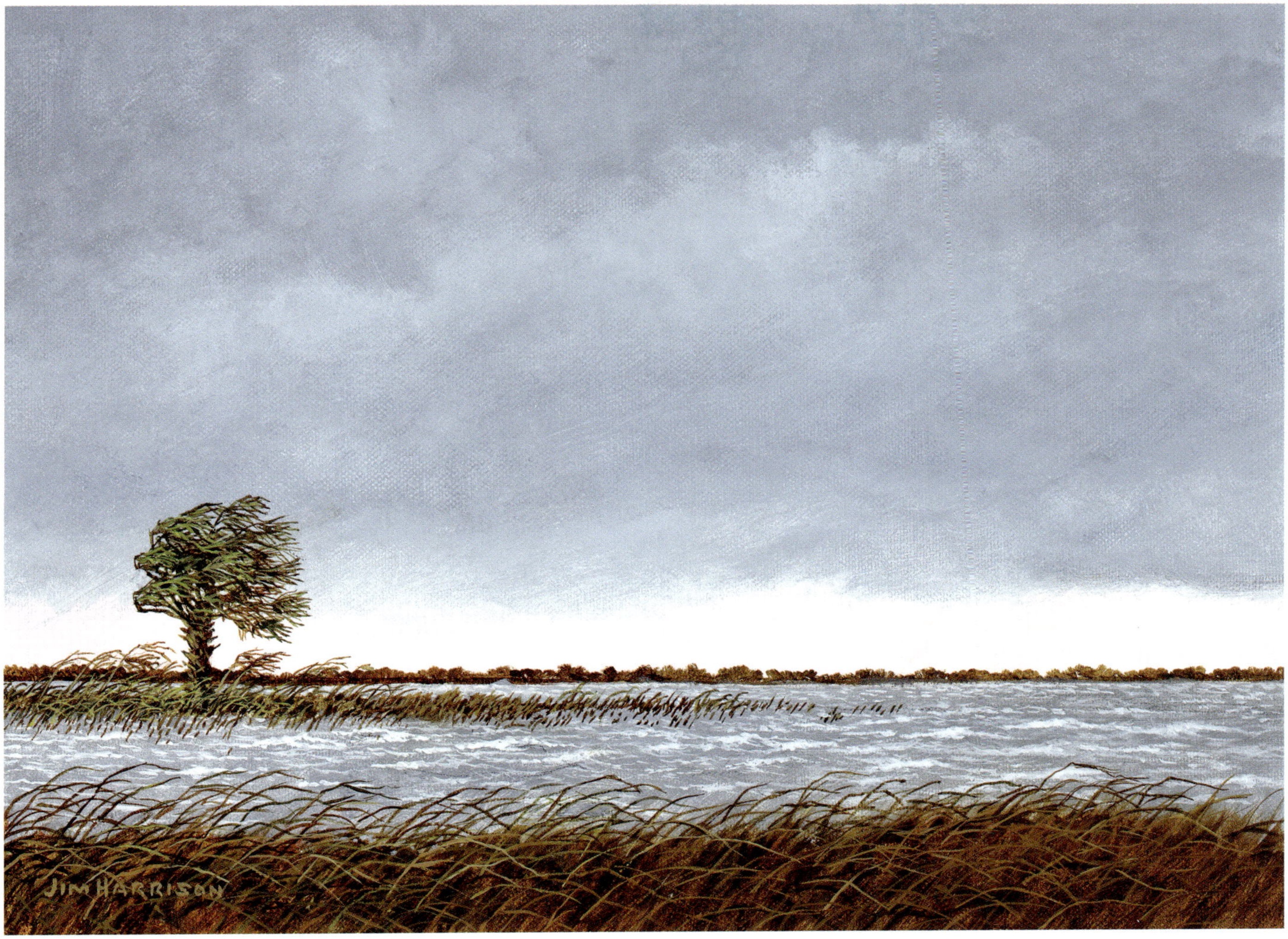

Stormy Palmetto

I HAVE ALWAYS HAD a hankering to go where one cannot or should not go. For example, I love the setting of the small hammock islands located in marshes, but I fear the reptiles that make their homes there. However, when I see a beautiful sunrise over the marshlands, I just can't resist getting as close to the islands and trees as my comfort zone will allow.

Overleaf: *Marsh*

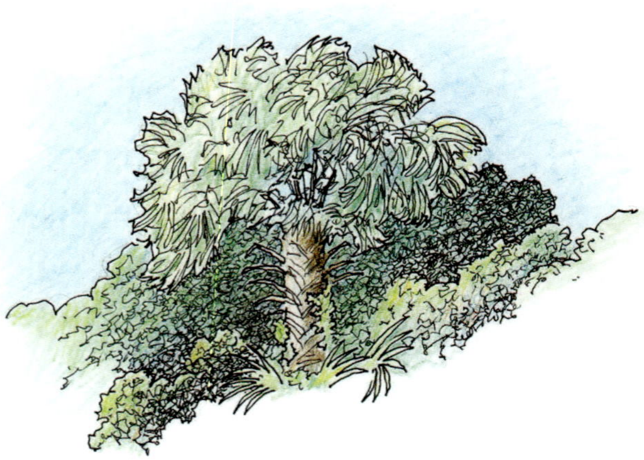

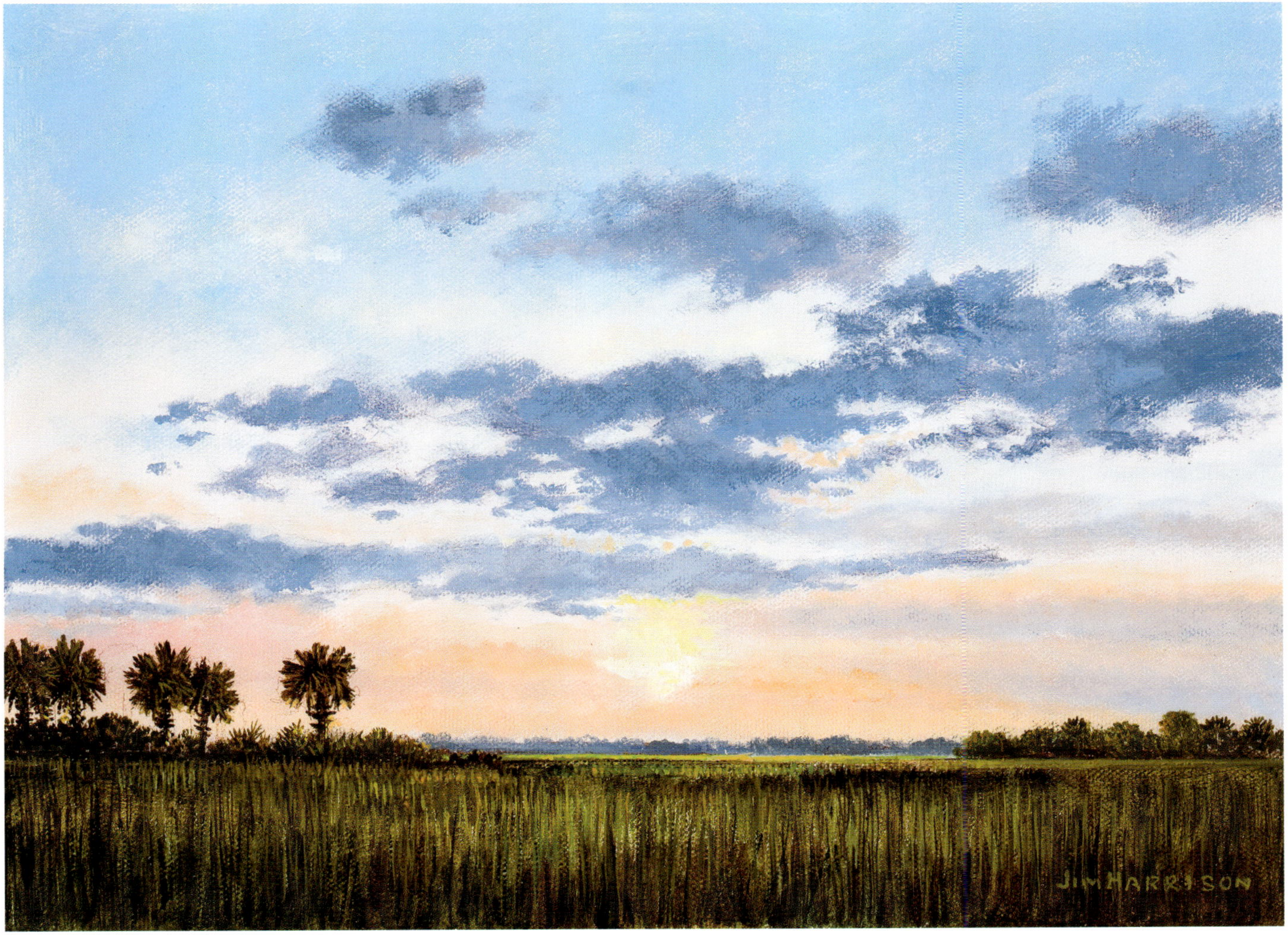

Palmetto Sunrise

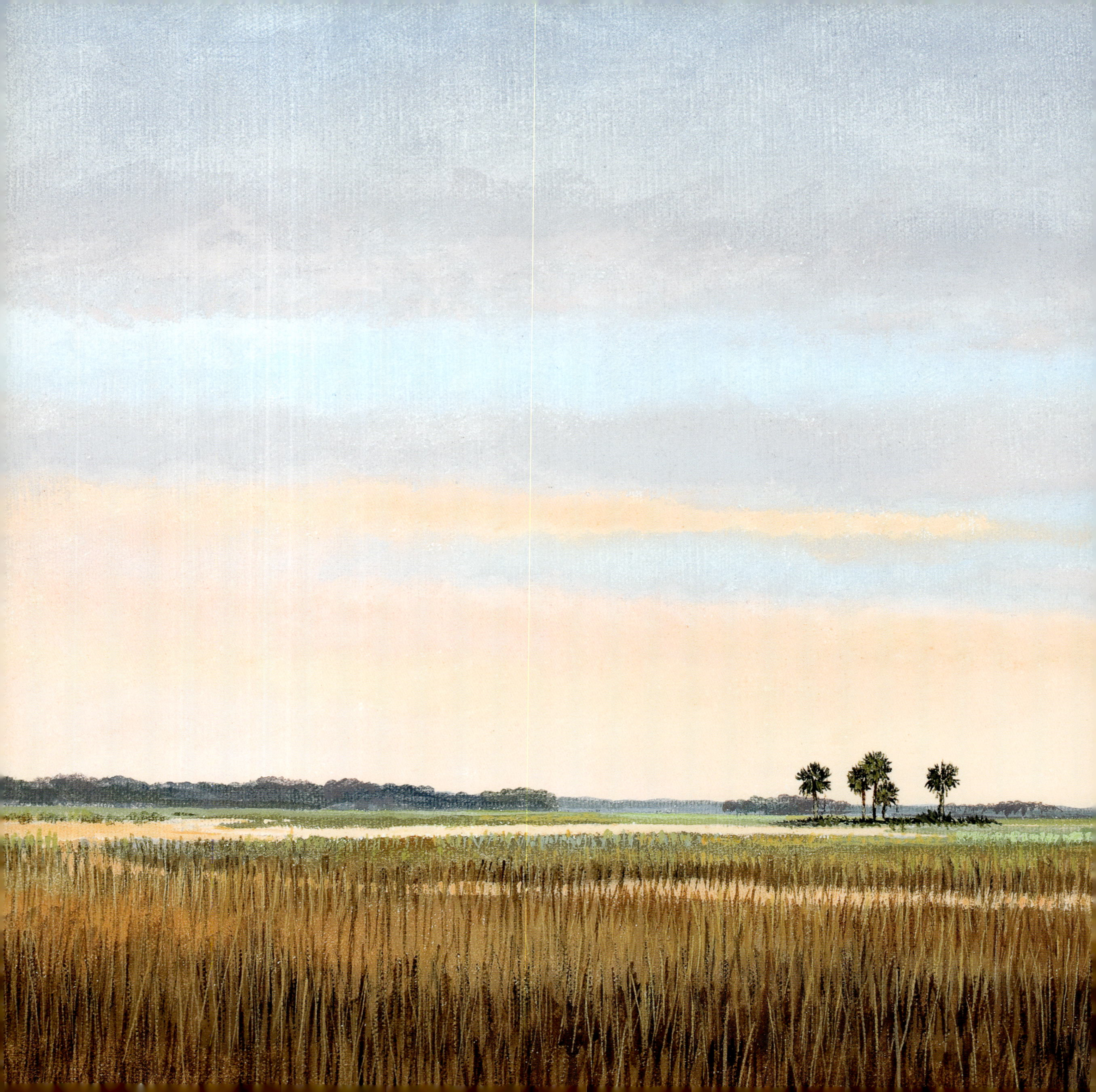

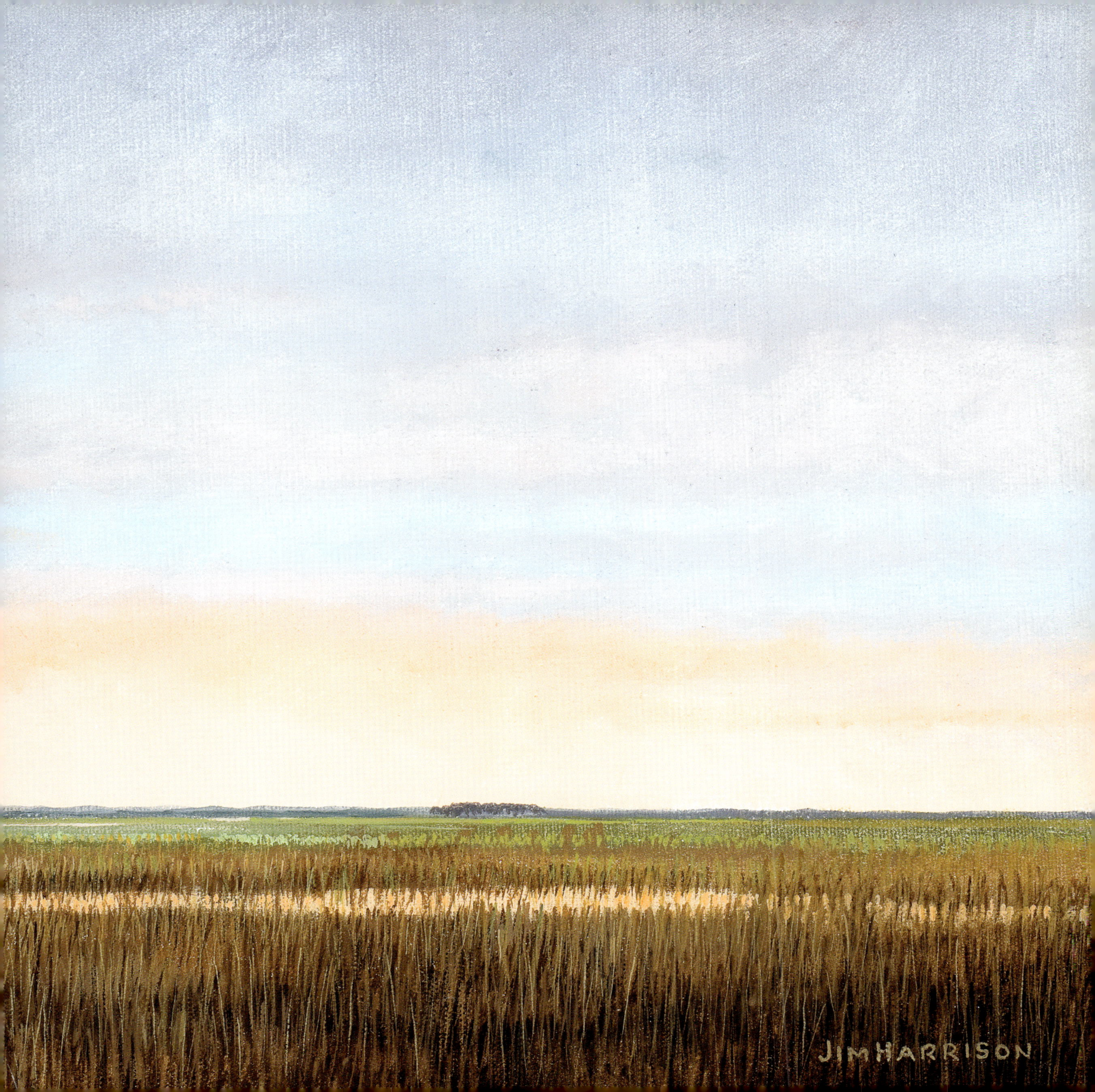
JIM HARRISON

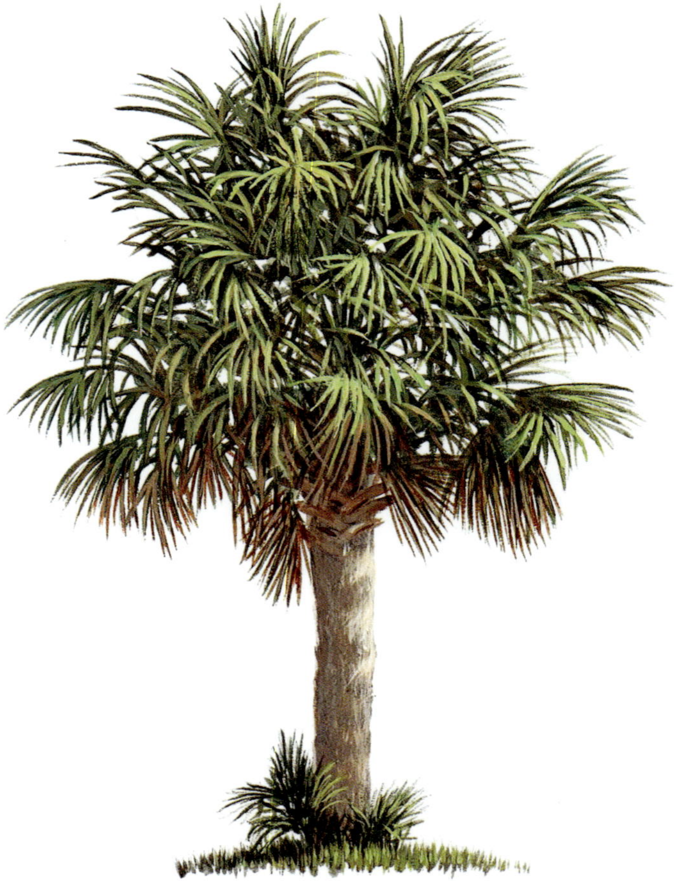

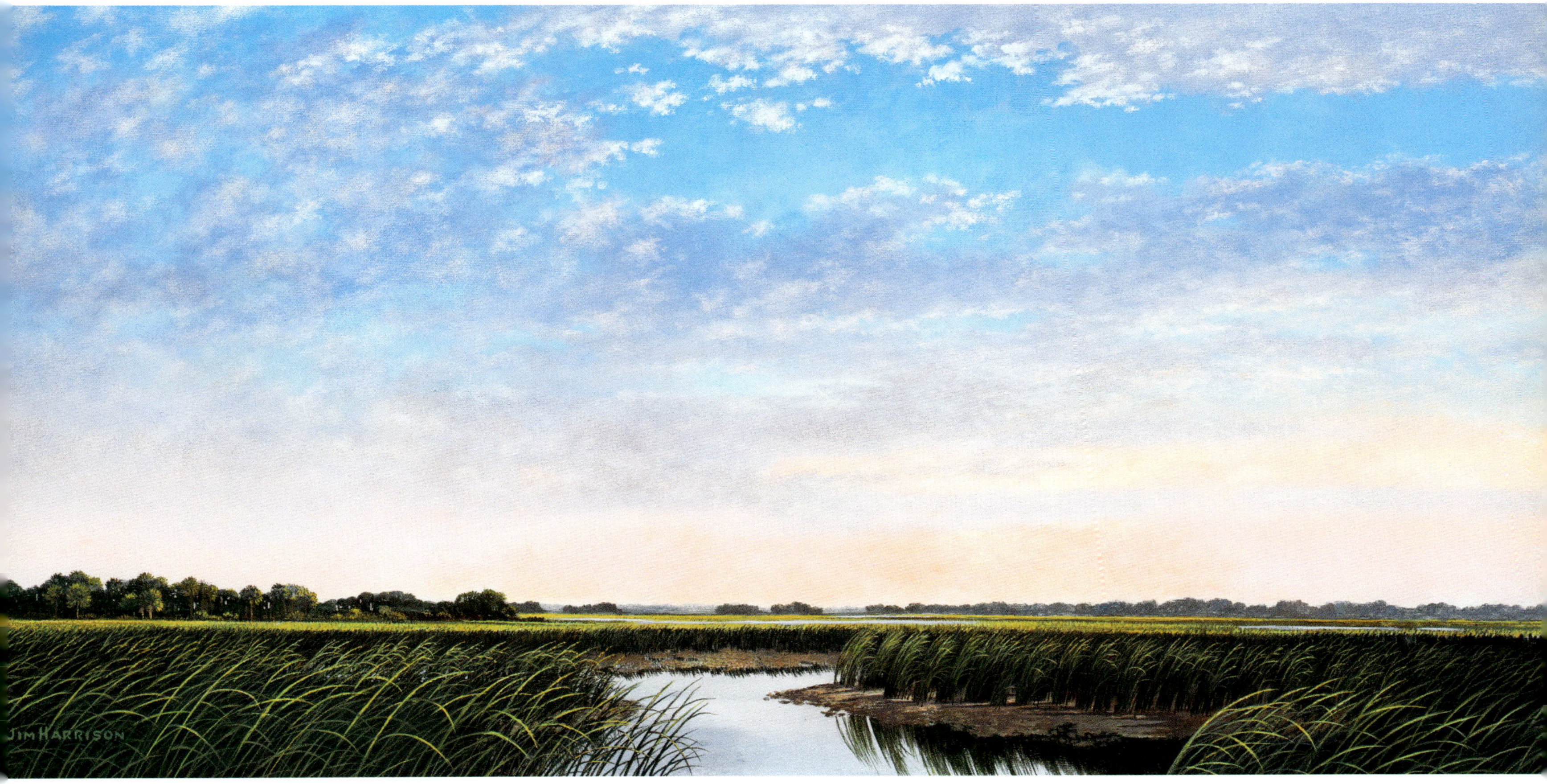

Marsh Creek

ON MANY A MORNING I have risen before the sun in order to see the light break through the low-lying clouds over the ocean's horizon. These ventures reward me with a myriad of colors that change by the second as the sunlight flits its way through the clouds to the earth below. The glistening water, sand, and palmetto trees provide a sight beyond compare.

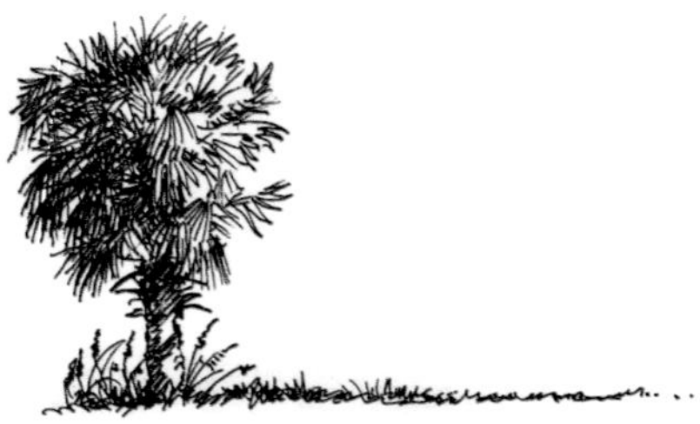

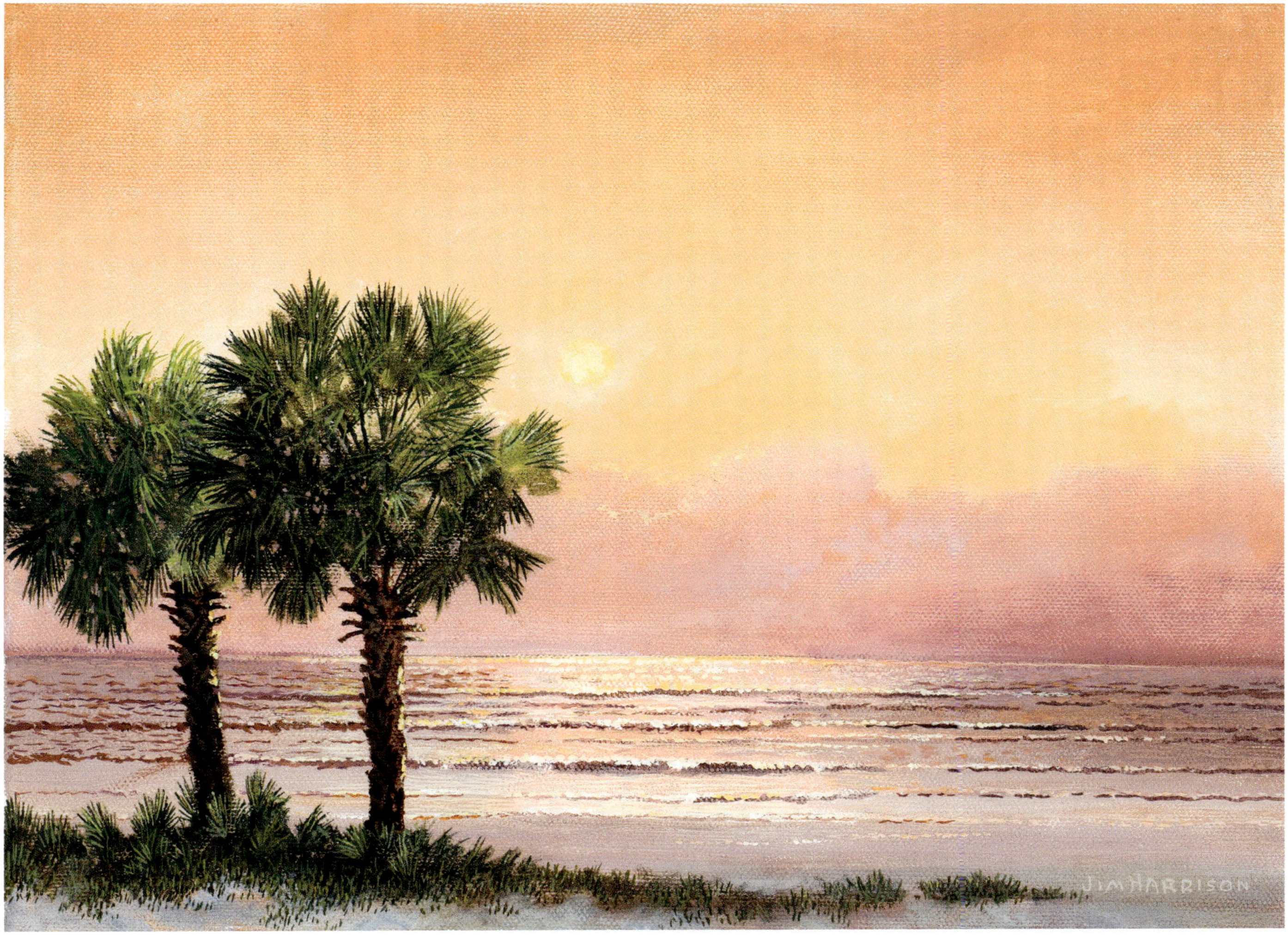

Palmetto and Sunrise

SUNSETS PROVIDE US with some of the most dramatic views of the sky, but the hues are constantly shifting. In my research I have hundreds of photographs, quick sketches, and notes for reference that enable me to try and paint the richness of the sun going down.

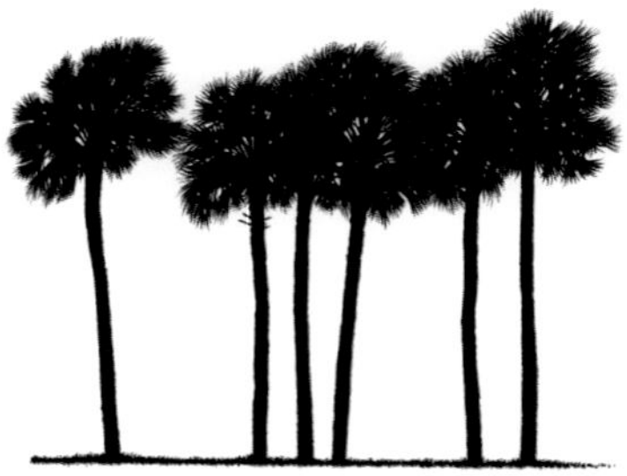

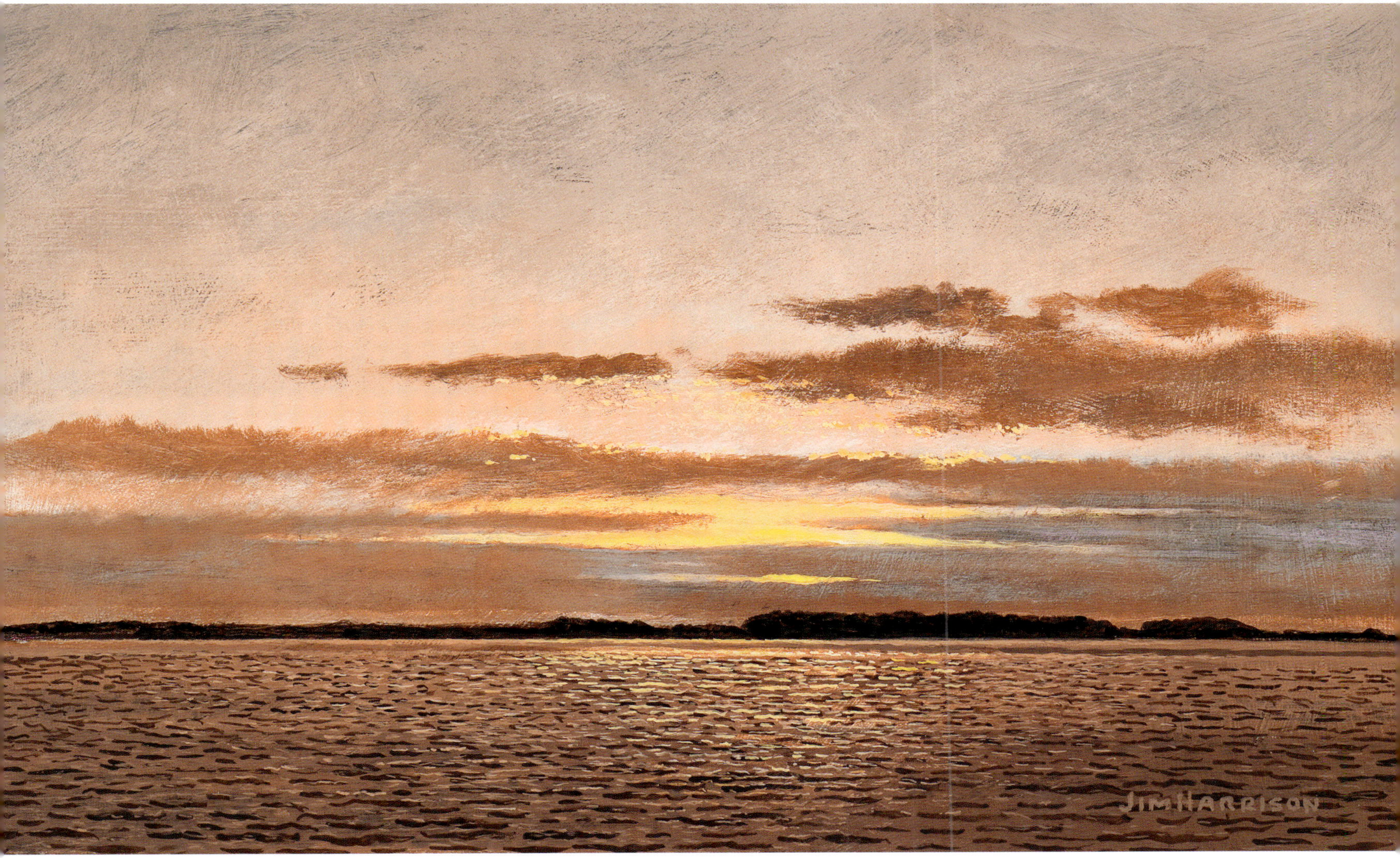

Orange and Brown Sunset

I ONCE WROTE FROM THE EDGE OF THE MARSH: "Sunsets do not shine, they leave a warm glow as they dance their way across and through trees and grass." At the horizon the sun's rays travel through more thickness of atmosphere and moisture than when the sun is overhead. The bending of the light influences the amount of reds and oranges that we see to create this warm glow. Even with all the observations I have made and all the photographs I have taken, it seems impossible to get the brilliance of color that exists. Sunsets are beautiful to look at and tough to paint.

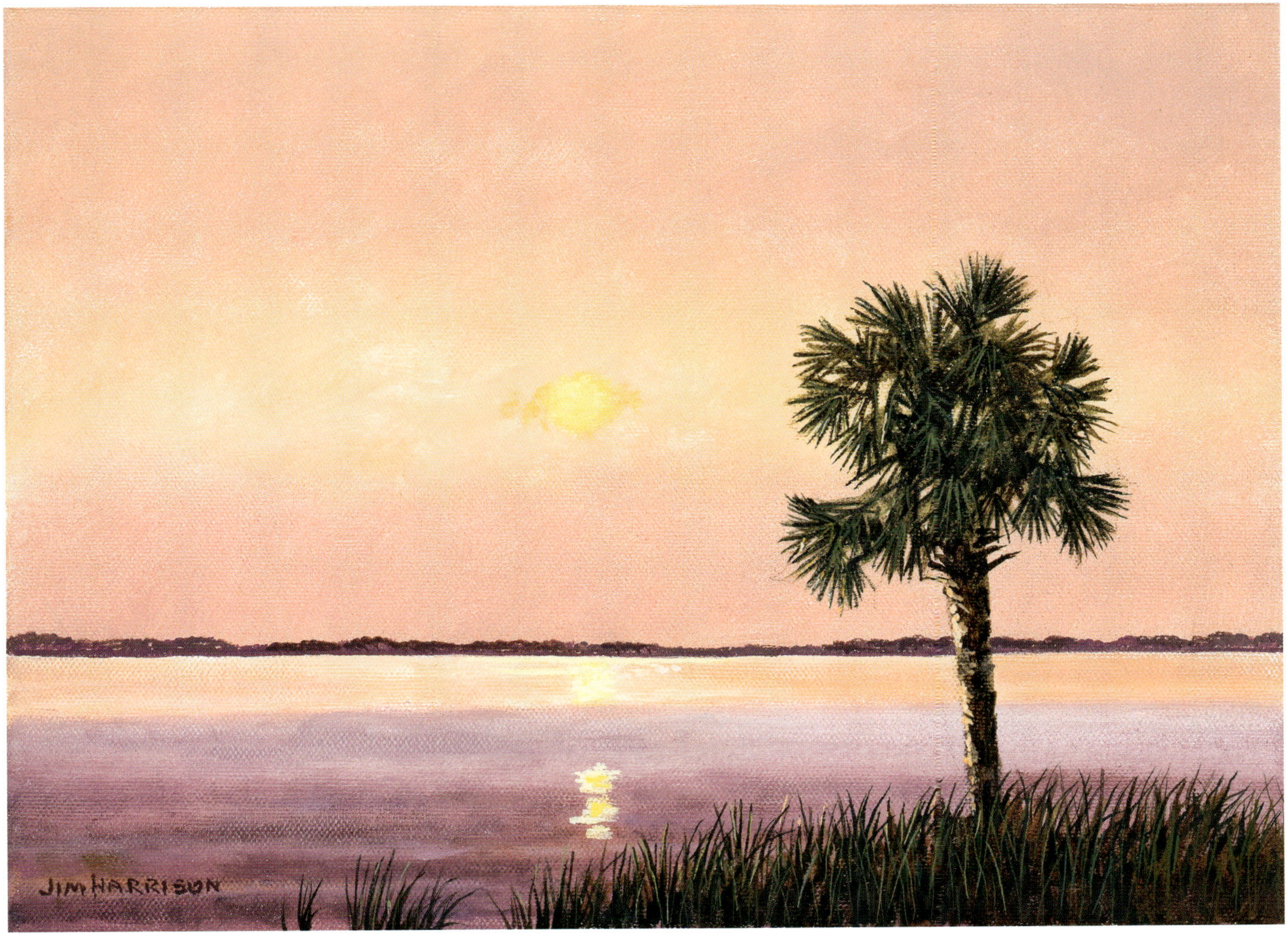

Palmetto Sunset

TO UNDERSTAND FULLY the growth characteristics of the palmetto tree I have, with the aid of a ladder, stuck my head right up among the fronds so I could actually see for myself the shape of the terminal bud and how it creates the new fronds.

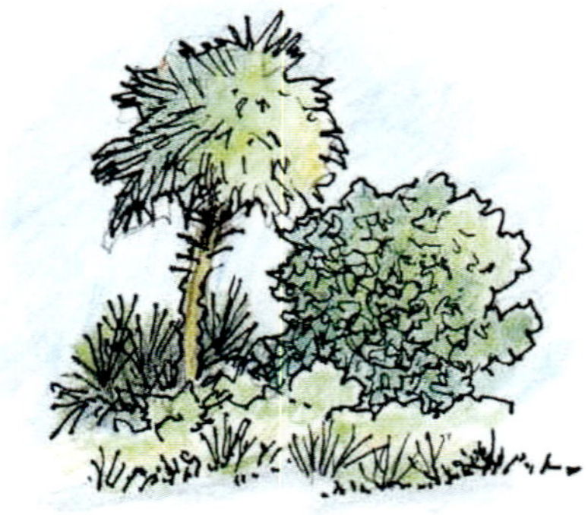

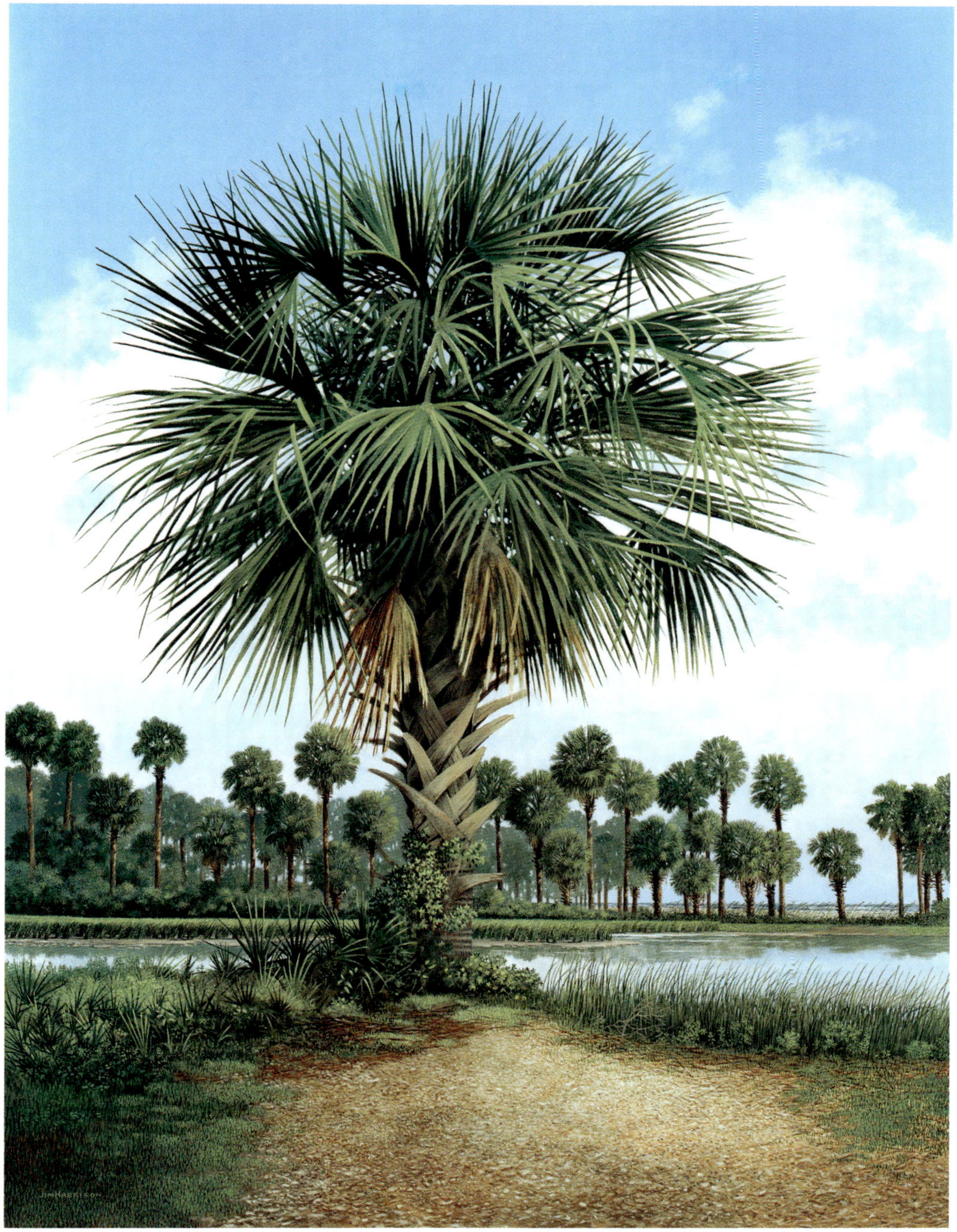

Palmetto Trees

THE COAST IS A SPECIAL PLACE, and South Carolina's is no exception. It beckons with southern warmth and hospitality. The graceful elegance of the seascape is even more enhanced by our beautiful state tree. There is nothing more tranquil to me than a deserted beach with a beautiful blue sky over calm water, white sand beneath my feet, and the presence of palmetto trees that tower above. These surroundings and moments give me a sense of peace, and I take pause to enjoy them every chance that I can get.

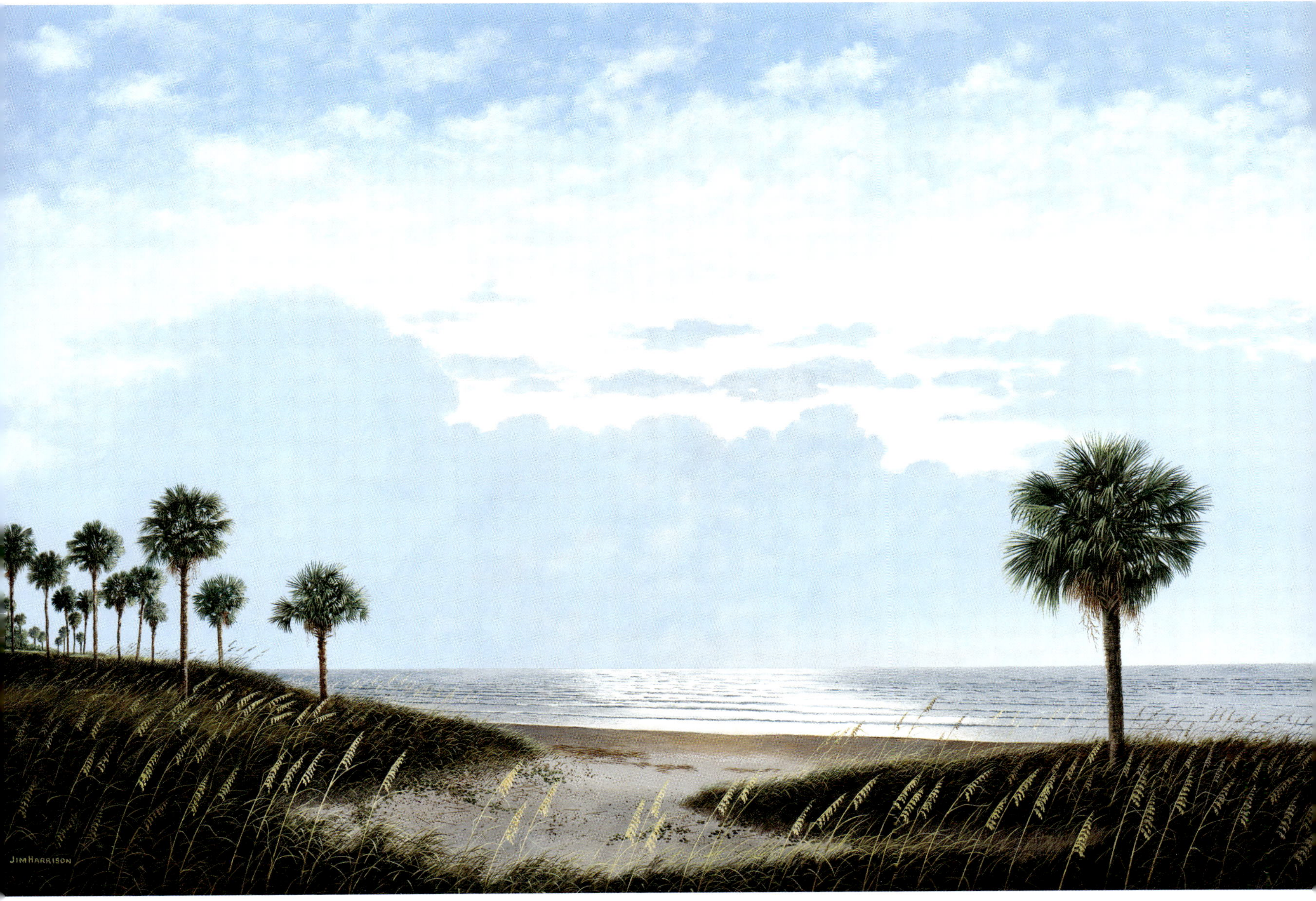

Palmettos

IF I HAD TO CHOOSE between watching the marsh or studying a path through the dunes to the beach, I am afraid my interest in the beach would come in second. I enjoy looking at the wetlands from the comfort of my car or from the safety of a large boat. From a distant vantage point, with the aid of a telescopic lens or binoculars, I study the character of the trees and grass. This allows me to see the many details of the foliage, palmetto trees, moss, and mud banks. Different compositions are sometimes hard to come by, and only by diligent observation can I get the fresh new look that I need to re-create the elements in my artwork.

Overleaf: *Storm Clouds over Marsh*

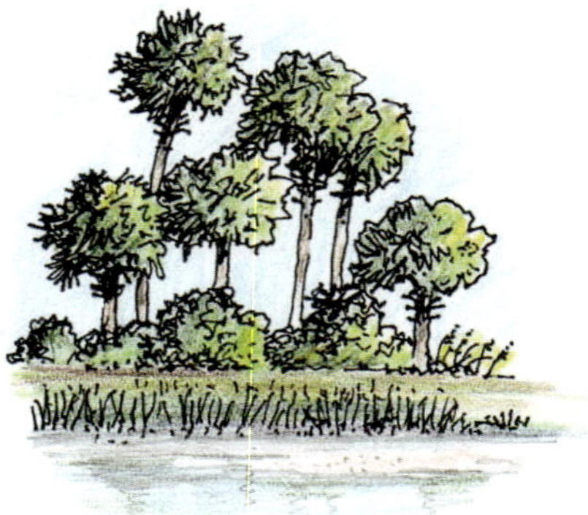

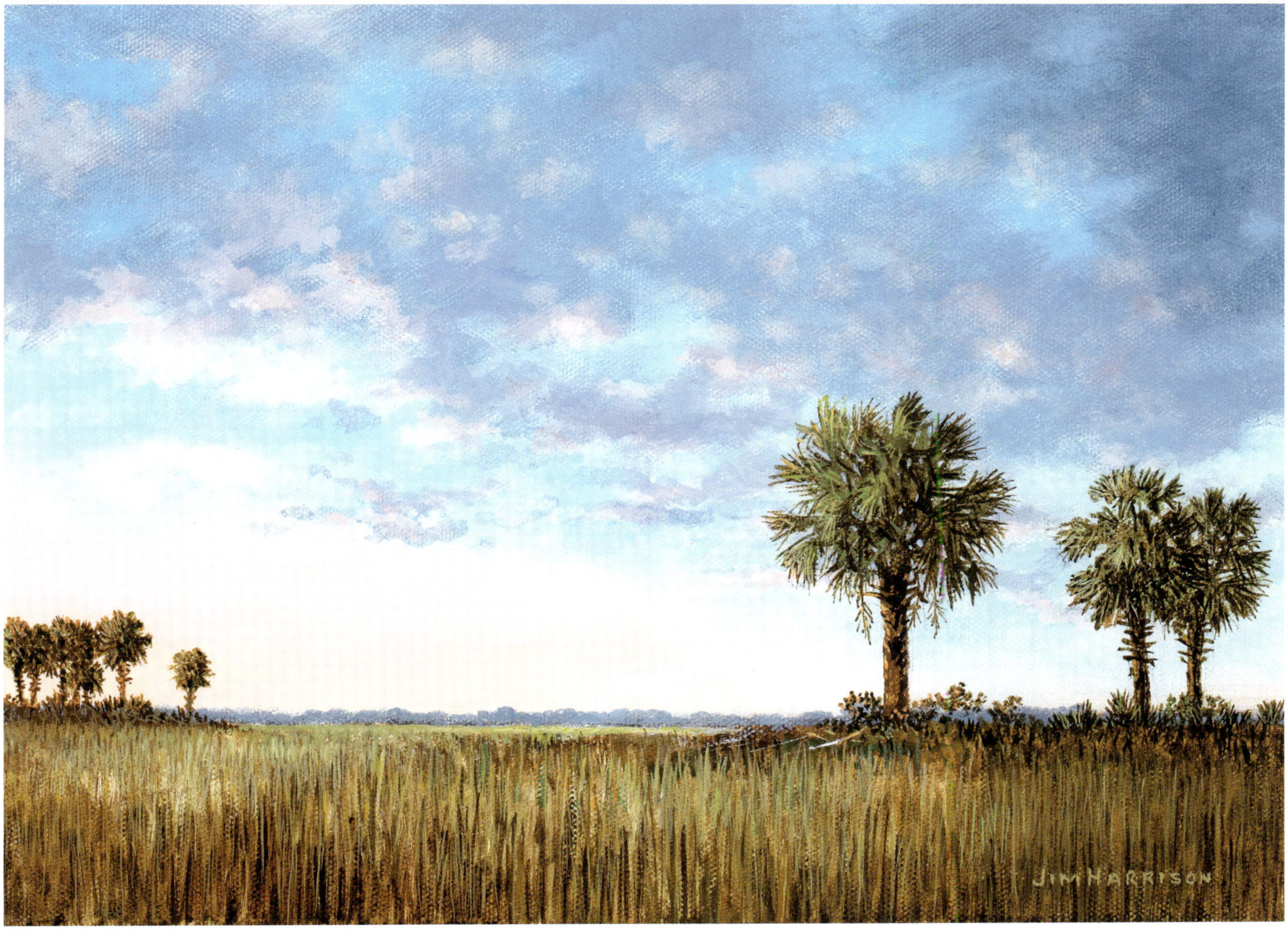

Palmettos and Marsh

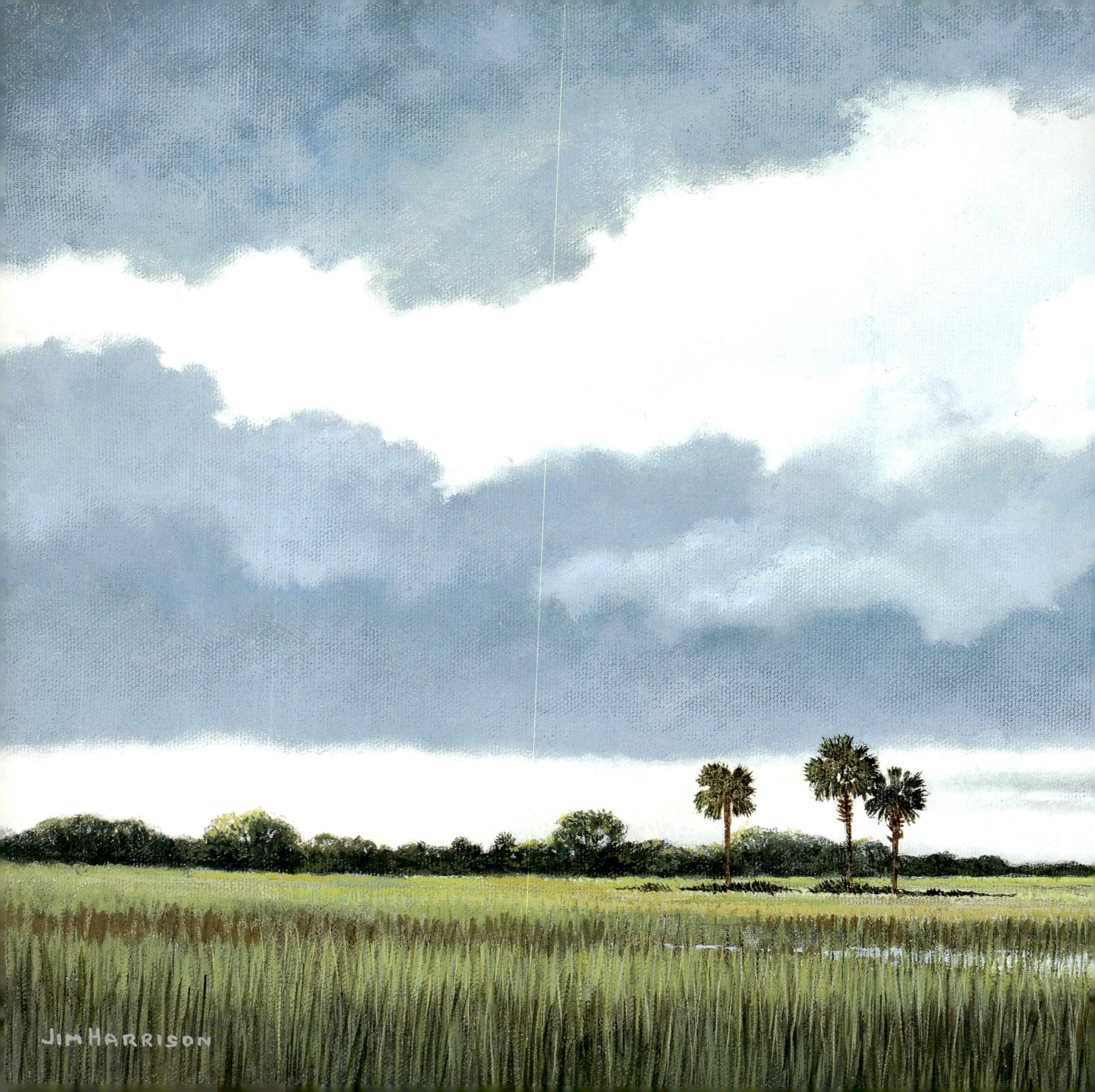
JIM HARRISON

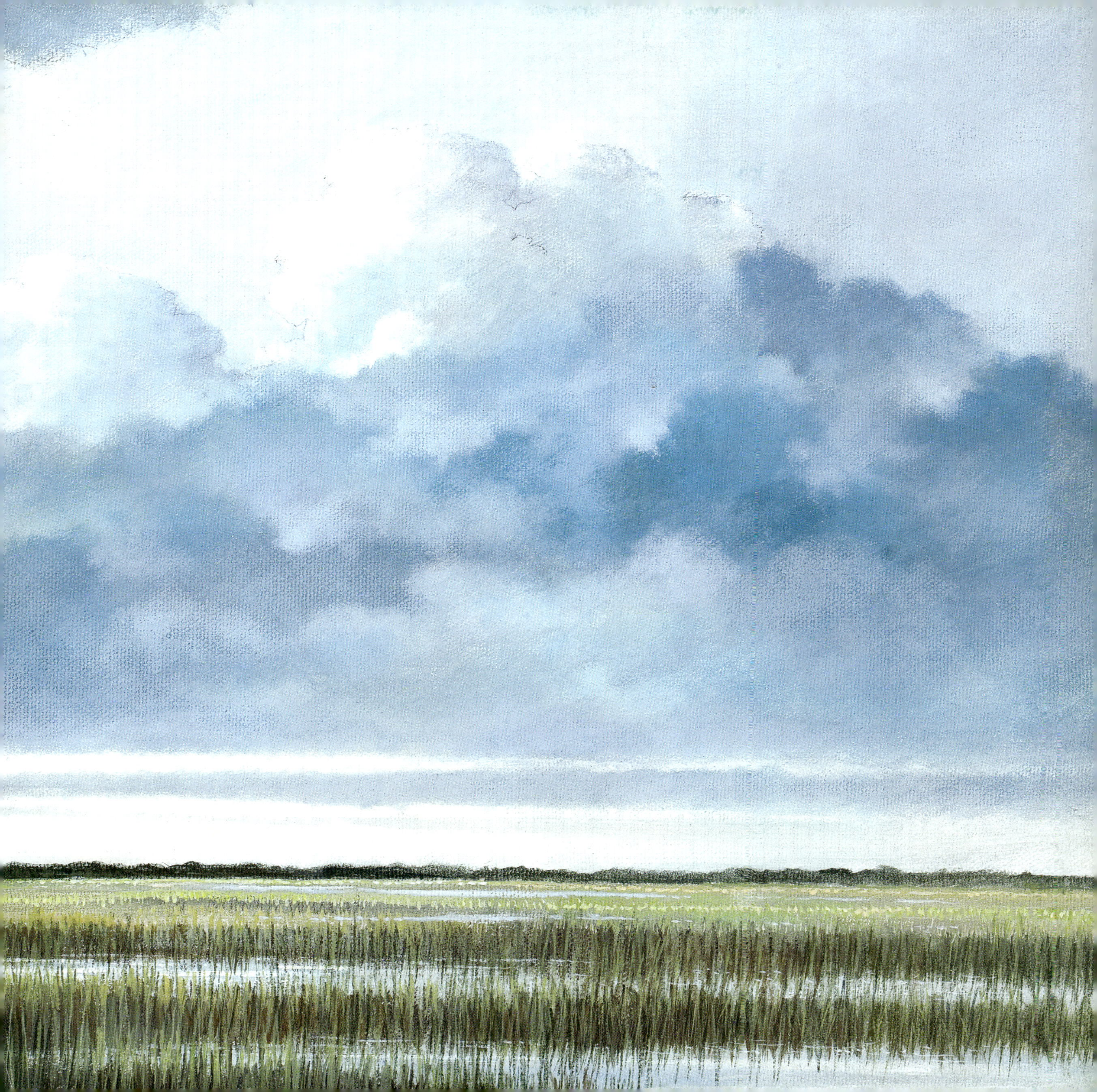

NEVER WILL I FORGET the beautiful summer day I headed out in a boat from the public landing near Beaufort, South Carolina. I traveled east along the northern edge of Port Royal Sound through Skull Creek to the end of Pritchards Island. It was then that I became aware of the vastness and beauty of the coastal marshes as well as the entire area where the land meets the sea. It was a "love at first sight" kind of thing that I knew was for real.

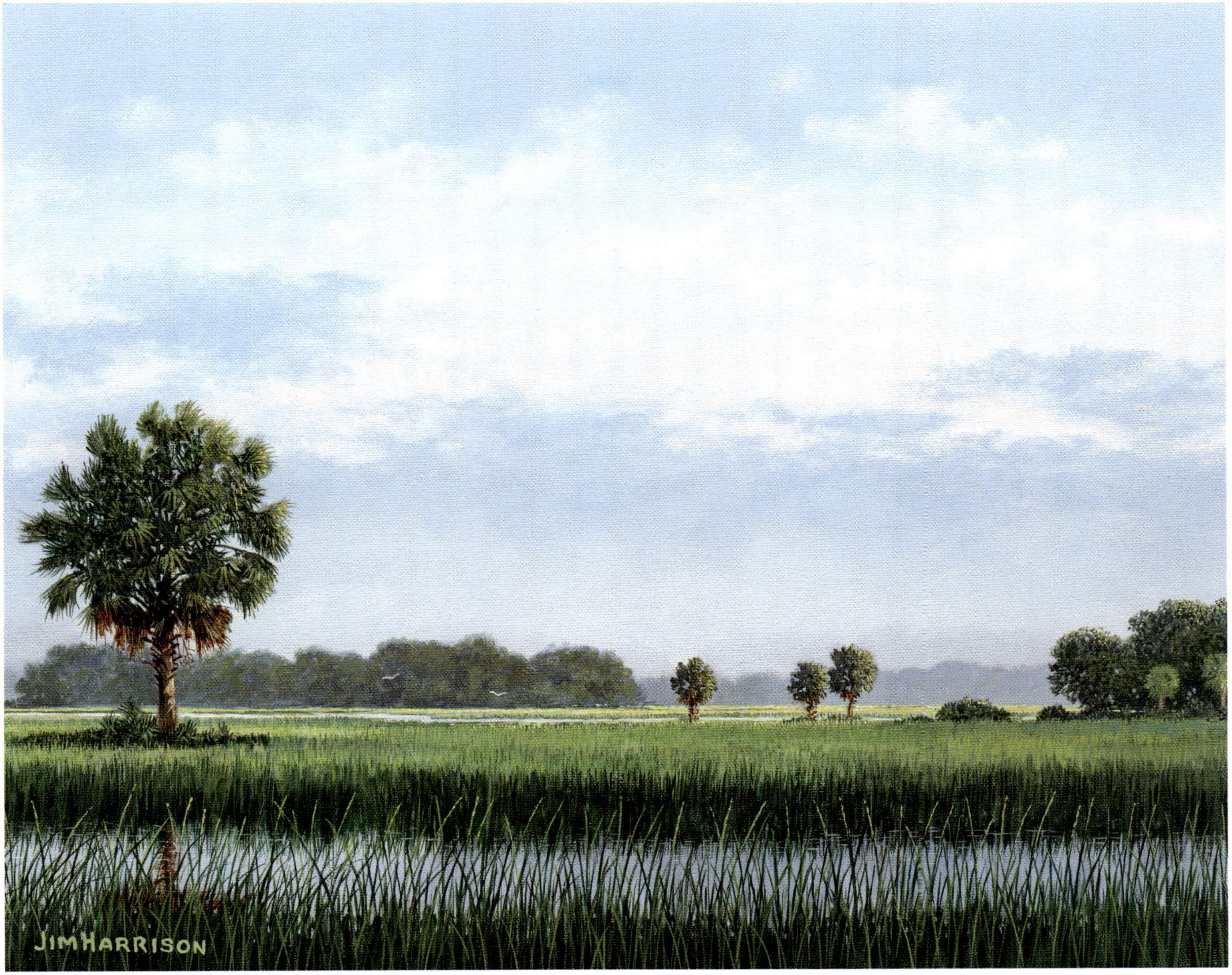

Palmettos in the Morning

FOR YEARS I HAVE STUDIED WAVES BREAKING ON THE BEACH, and often I spent hours out in the surf, sitting in a chair, watching and trying to follow the movement of the water as it rushed up to the sand and trees. The meeting of water, sand, grass, and trees is one subject that I paint without full knowledge of what is really happening, but I have come to appreciate the beauty of that space that is neither land nor sea.

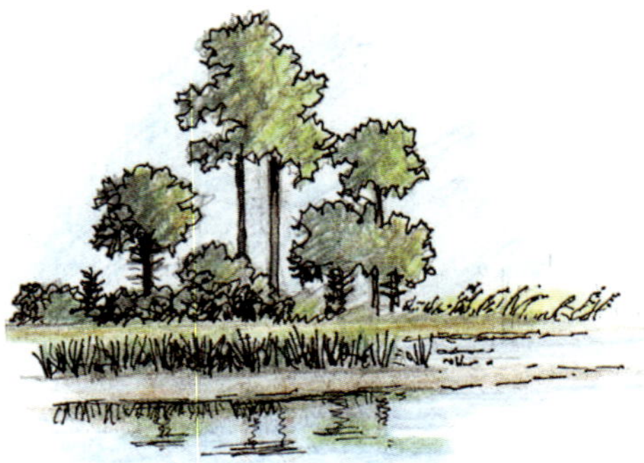

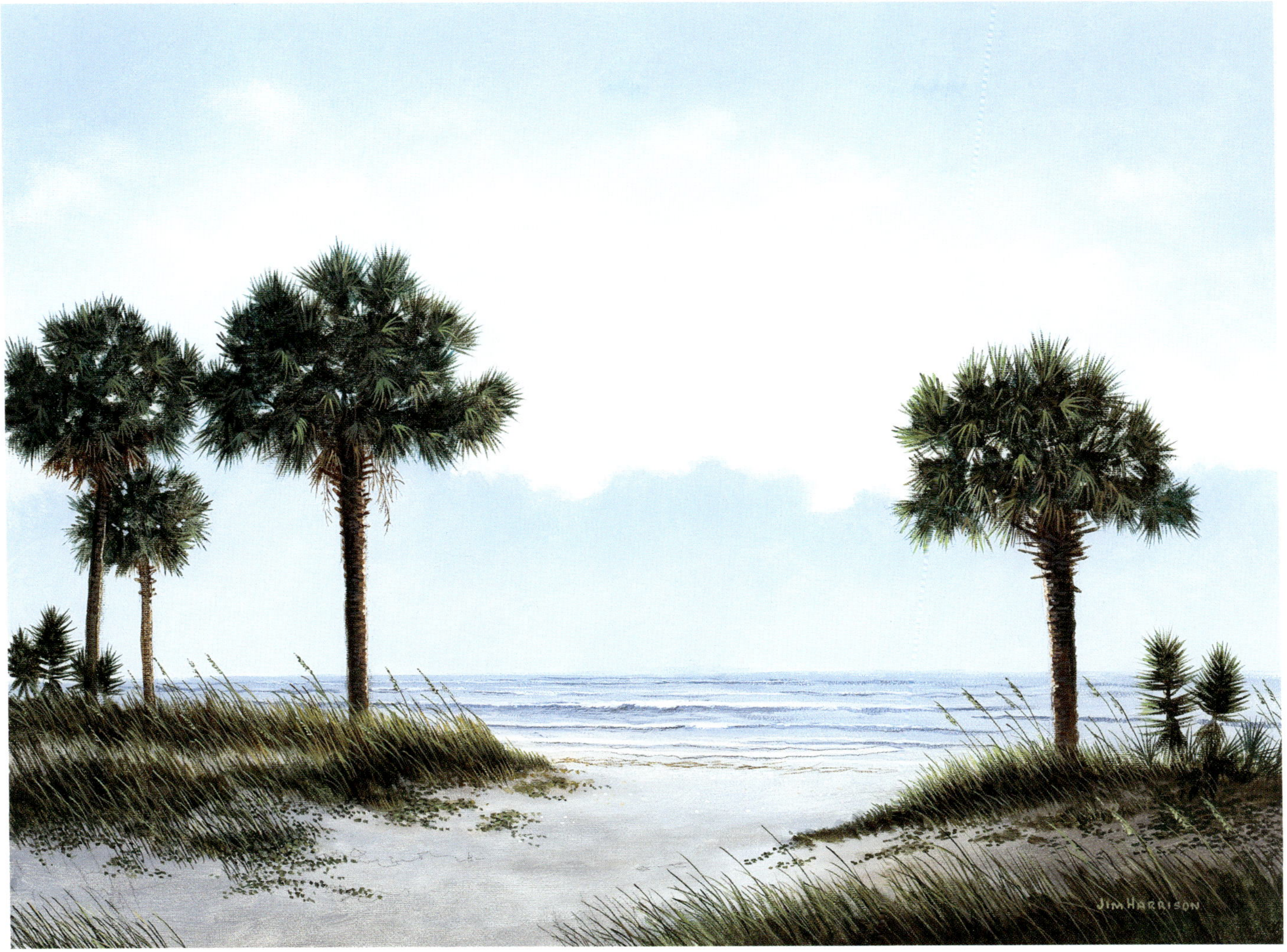

The Palmettos

VERY LITTLE OF OUR AMERICAN HERITAGE, including our beaches, coastal marshes, and the trees along them, remains unspoiled by pollution or undamaged by the bulldozer. It is my hope to stay a little ahead of the wrecking crews so that I may record as much about these places as possible.

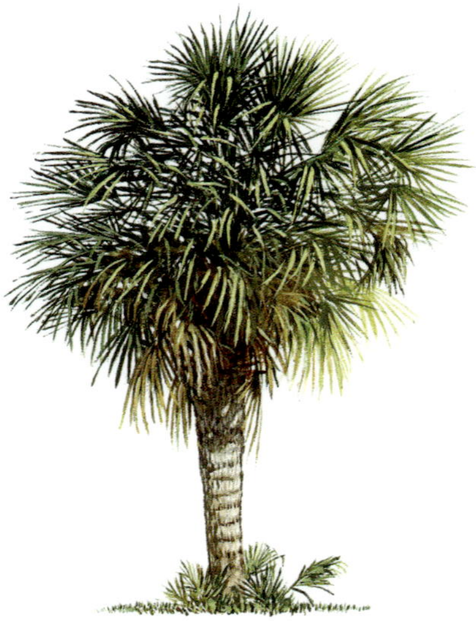

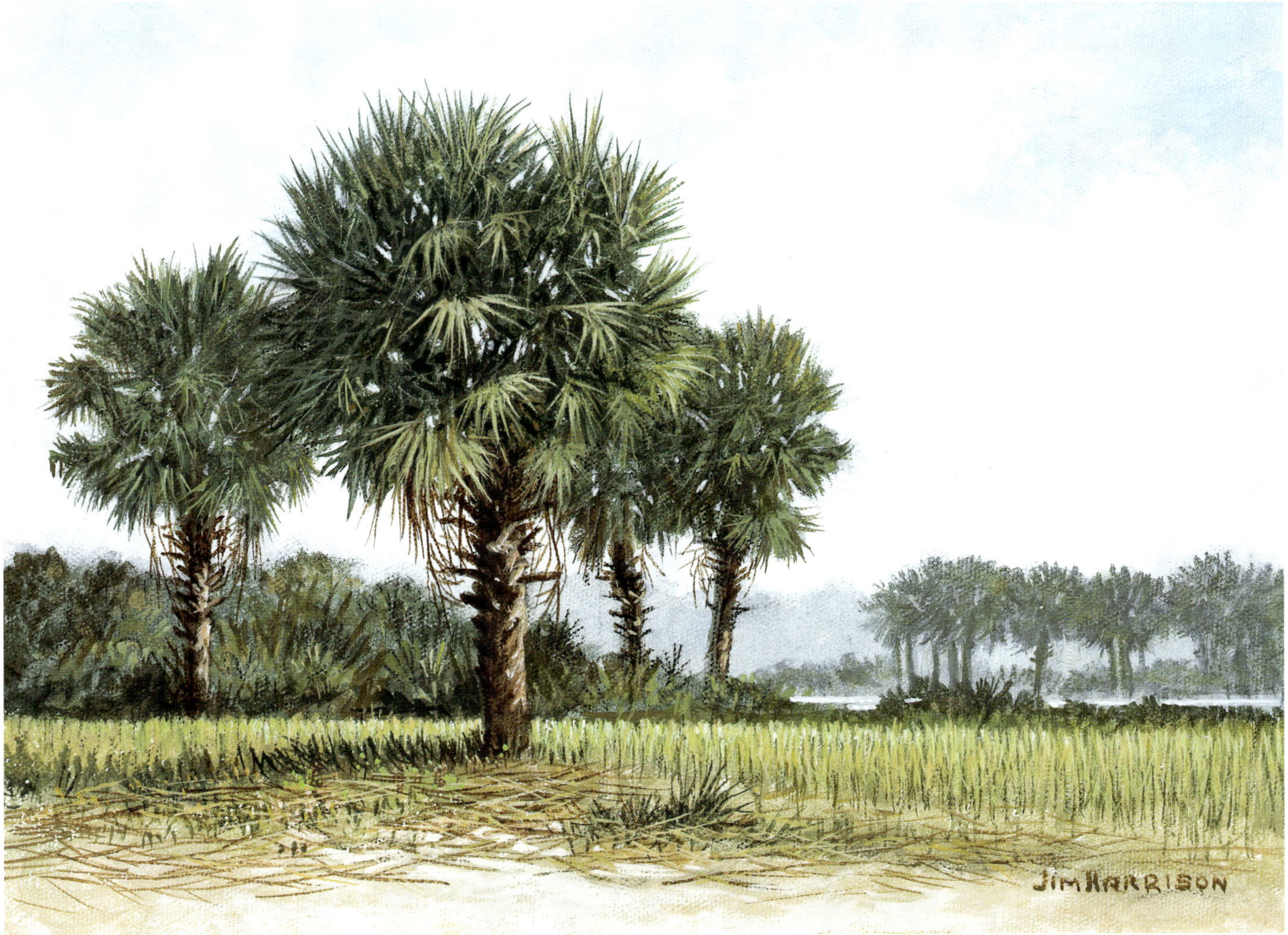

Palmettos in the Sand

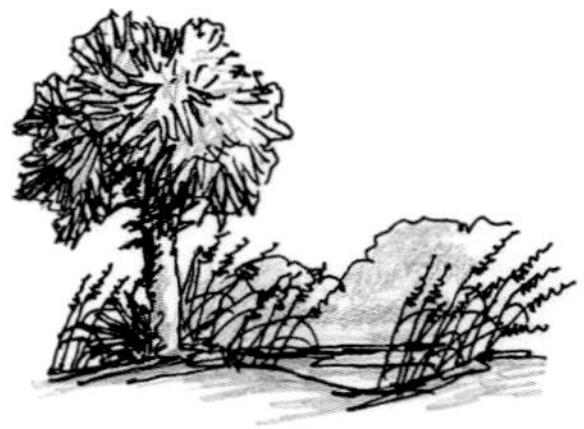

ON A CLEAR DAY one can focus on the beach or trees in the near foreground, and they are very distinct, while at the same time the distant horizon is fuzzy and vague. Yet the observer can look up to focus on the horizon, which then is a distinct straight line and the nearby plant life is fuzzy and out of focus. This requires me to be aware constantly of a focal point—here, the palmetto trees—and emphasize that point by blurring the rest of the picture.

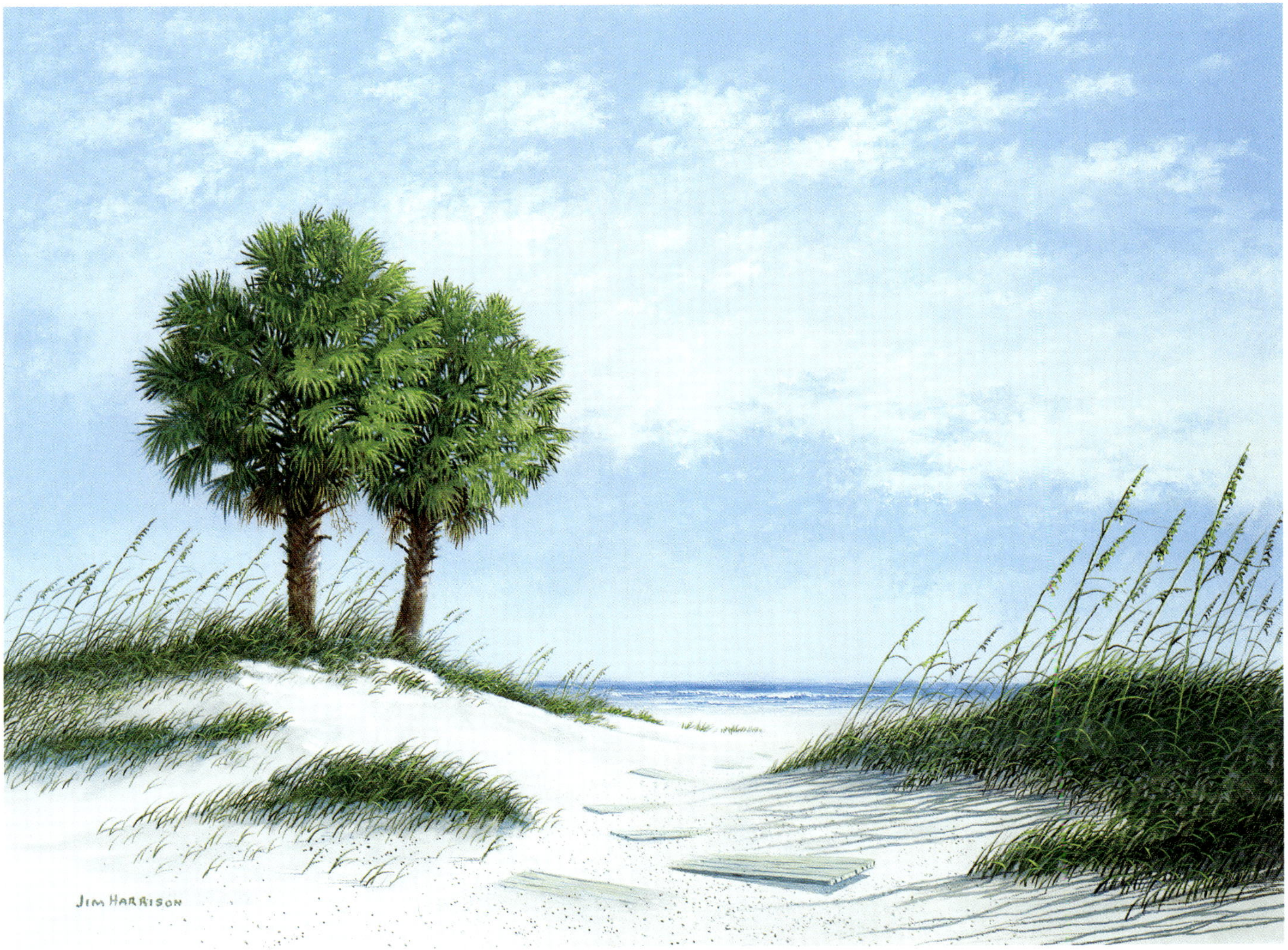

Palmettos in Dunes

MY EARLY ATTEMPTS at painting beach sand involved Paynes gray mixed with white and black. But beach sand has small pieces of broken shells and grit mixed in with it, making it a combination of a multitude of colors. I learned too that shadows should be cool and the sunlight warm. So I added a purple to the shadows and used more raw sienna and yellow ochre to warm up the sunny areas. This emphasis on shadows and on the ground beneath the palmettos helps to bring out the nuances of light and dark that every tree has.

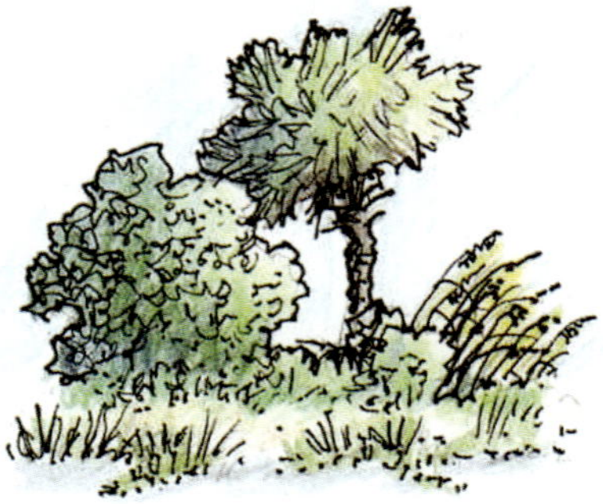

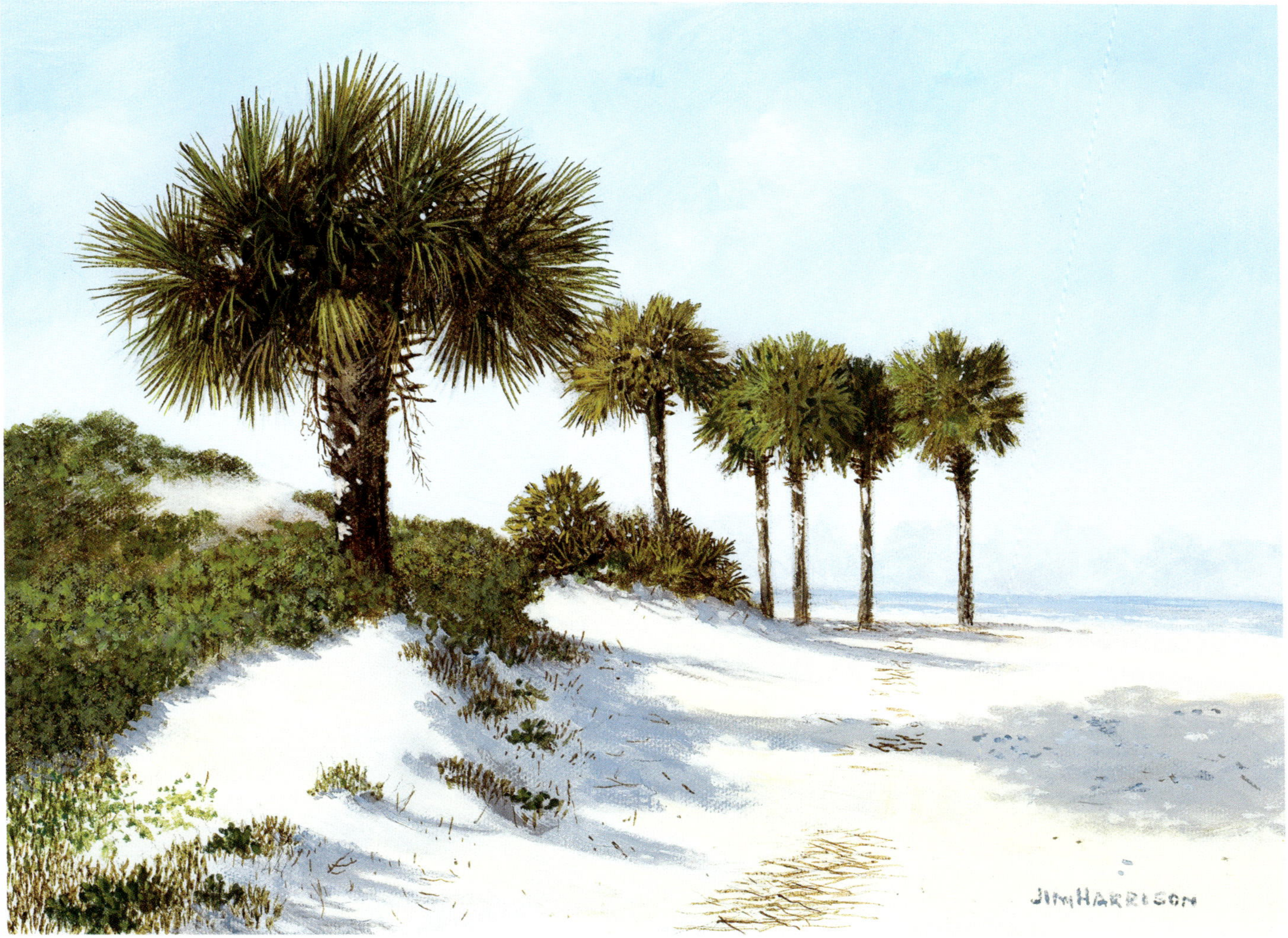

Dunes and Palmettos

SOUTH CAROLINA IS SUCH A BEAUTIFUL STATE. I truly believe that part of my job as an artist is to draw attention to the common things that we don't always view as beautiful, important, or unique. And if that means my work causes you to enjoy the sky, water, and trees in a way that you haven't before, then I think I've done my job well.

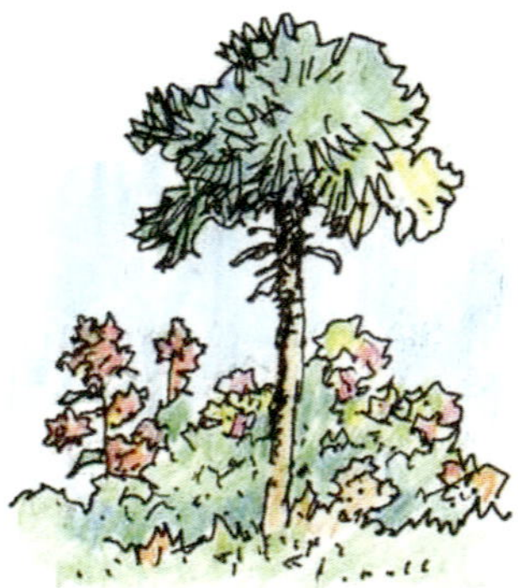

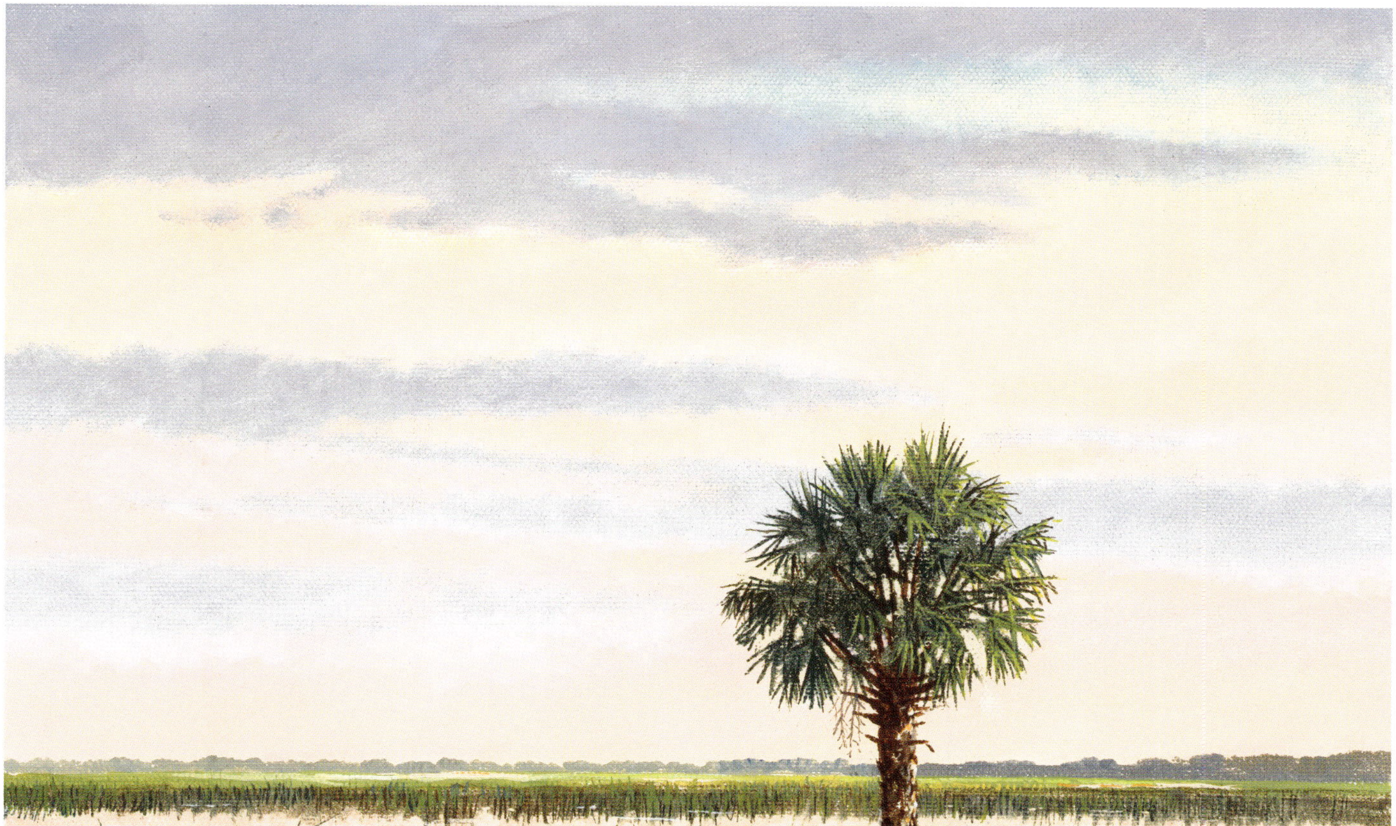

Sky and Palmetto

AS A YOUNGSTER, I was taken by my mama and daddy, along with my two brothers, on day trips to Edisto Beach State Park. We were usually quite excited until about noon, when we were all blistered and salty, in search of a shower, and ready to eat lunch. Sometimes we ate under the shade of a tree, but more often I recall eating in the picnic areas that were under shelters with thatched roofs much like the ones Indians used to make. I remember once being amazed during a downpour that the palmetto roof did not leak.

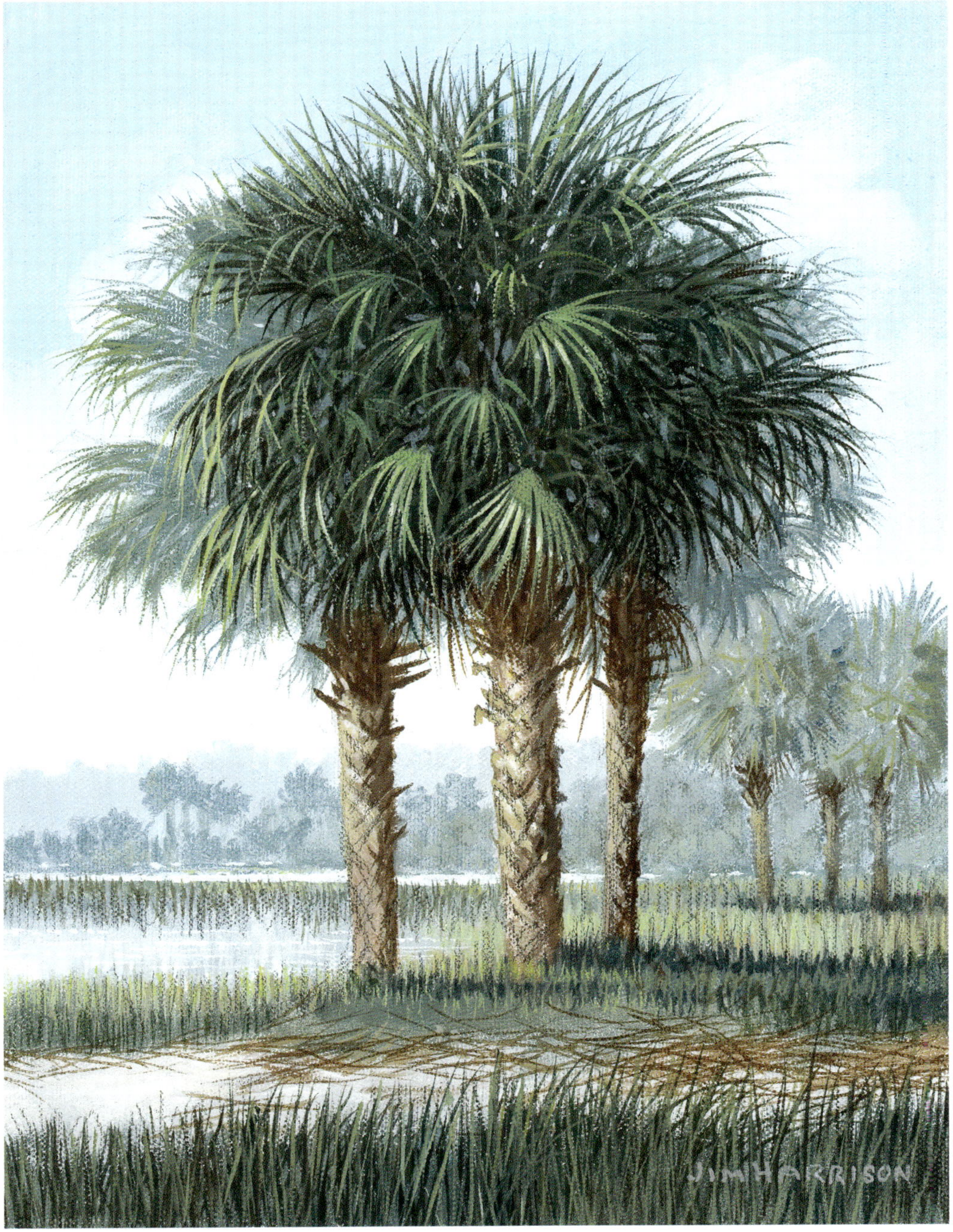

Three Palmettos

WE ARE ACCUSTOMED TO including things we cherish in our Christmas decorating traditions. For some this may include hanging ornaments on a palmetto and placing gifts under it for those passing by to see and appreciate. We South Carolinians surely do love our palmetto trees, no matter what time of year it is.

Below: *Palmetto Christmas 2007*

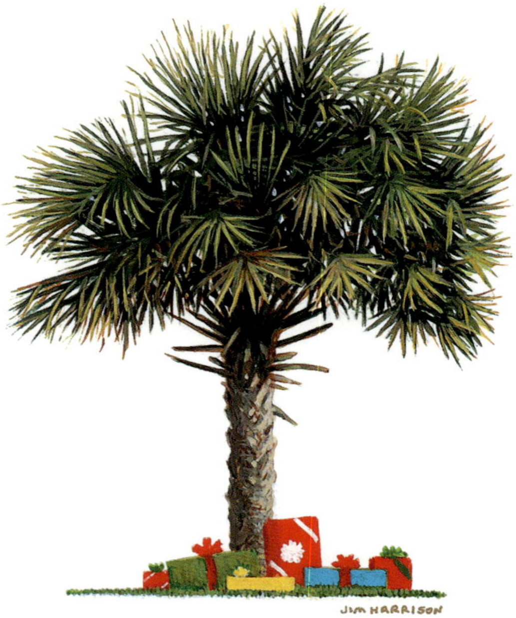

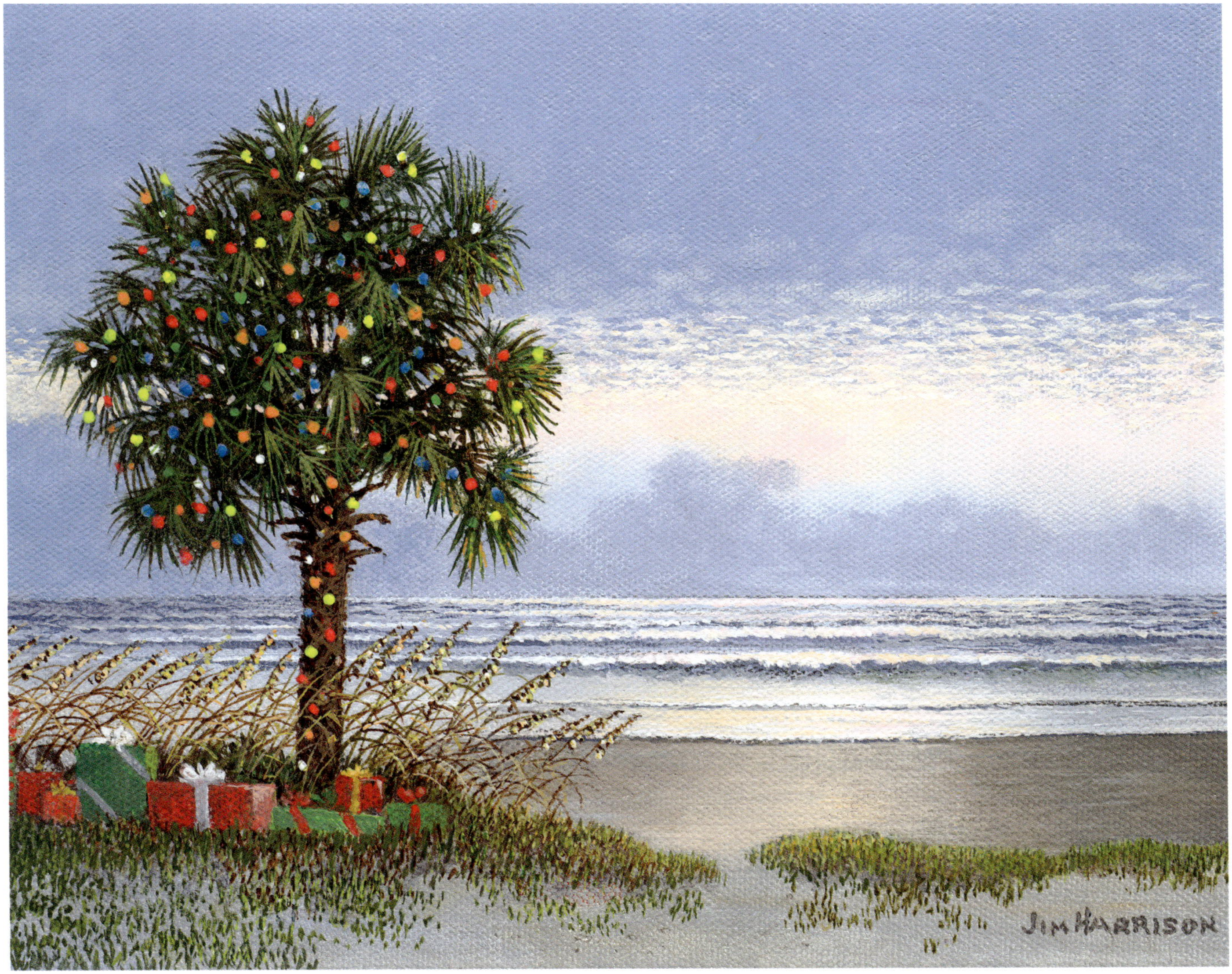

Palmetto Christmas 2008

I HAVE HEARD STORIES of South Carolinians who include palmetto trees in their Christmas decorating. I have not seen them so I am not sure that is true, but if it has not happened, it certainly should. With my palmetto Christmas cards, I am in no way suggesting that we adopt the palmetto as our Christmas tree. I intend no irreverence toward the sanctity of Christmas, and I mean no disrespect for the dignity of South Carolina's state icon.

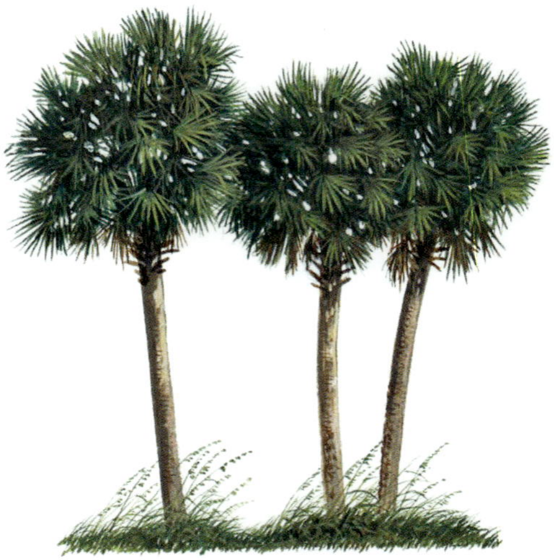

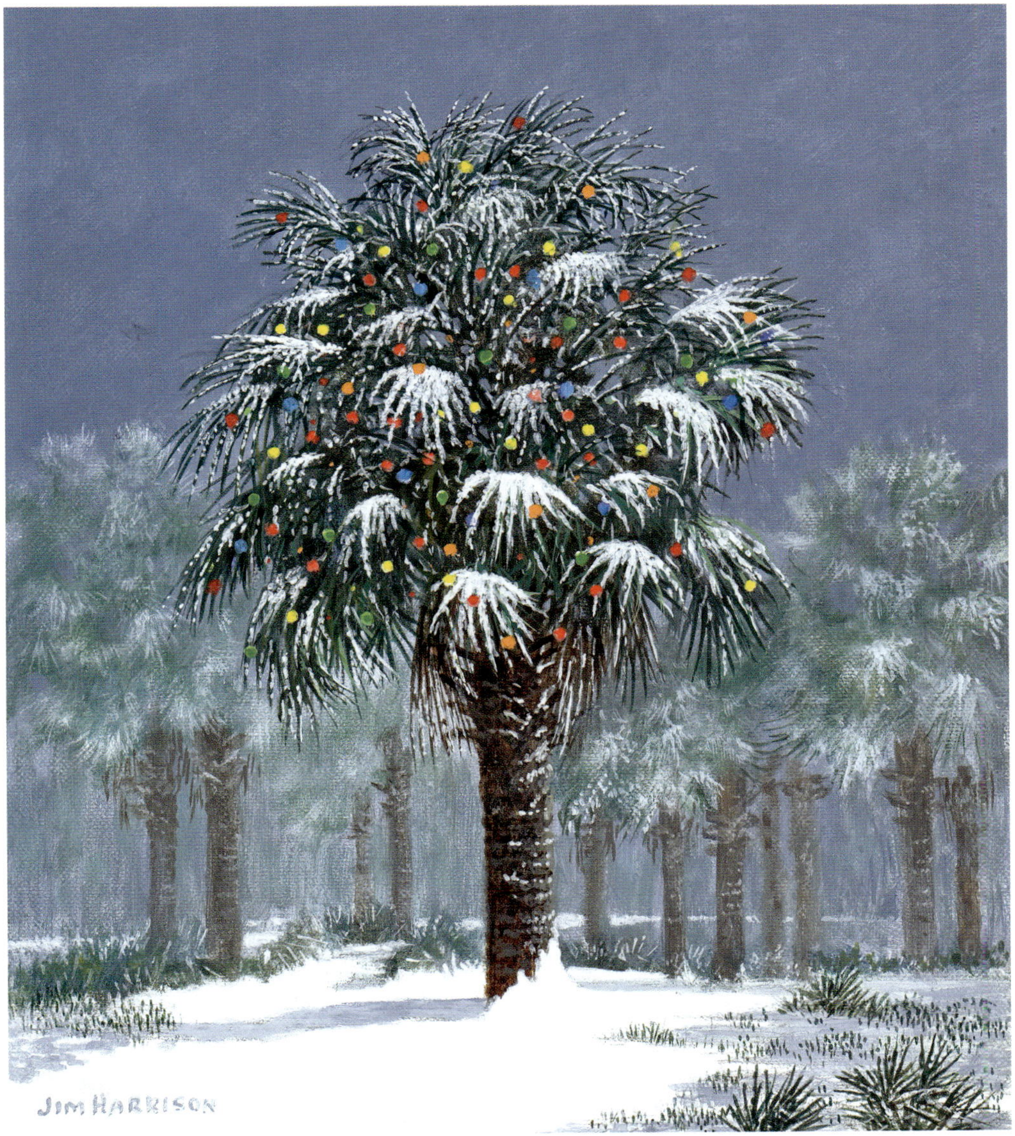

Palmetto Christmas 2009

WE JUST CAN'T SEEM TO GET ENOUGH of the palmetto tree image in pop culture these days. The hearty tree has become an icon that is well loved by many South Carolinians and others.

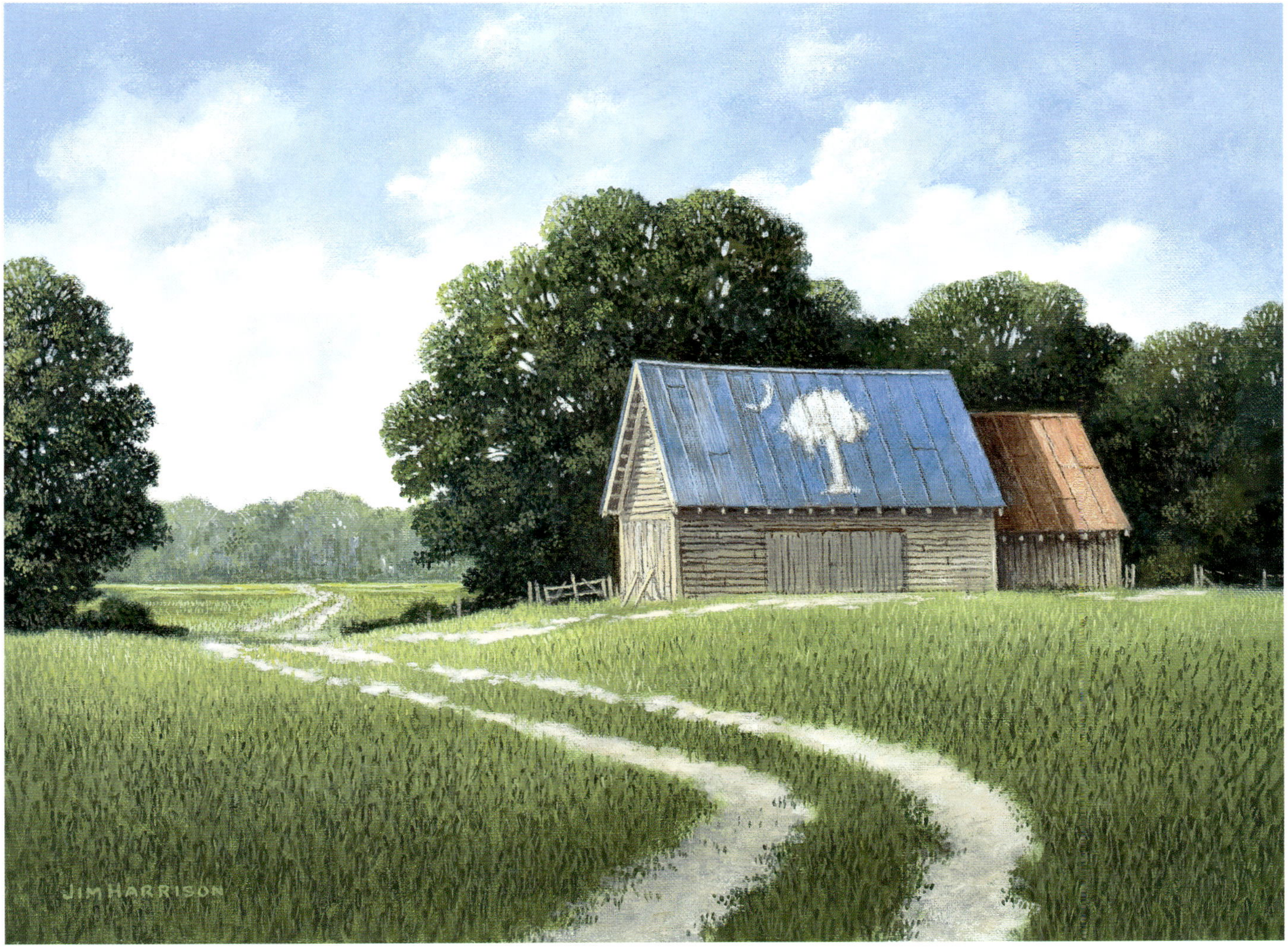

Palmetto Barn

South Carolina's Fascination with the Palmetto Tree

THE PALMETTO WAS ADOPTED as the "Official State Tree of the State of South Carolina" by Joint Resolution No. 63, approved March 17, 1939, by the South Caroline legislature. The palmetto tree is also represented on the state flag, state seal, and state quarter, thanks to its historic role in the American Revolution.

Asked by the Revolutionary Council of Safety in the fall of 1775 to design a flag for the use of South Carolina troops, Col. William Moultrie chose a blue that matched the color of their uniforms and a crescent that reproduced the silver emblem worn on the front of their caps. In the years to come, South Carolina needed a national flag after it seceded from the Union. The General Assembly considered a wide range of designs but in January 1861 added the palmetto to Moultrie's original design.

The palmetto continues to be a prominent feature of the state flag even today, and South Carolina is known as the Palmetto State. The salute to the flag of South Carolina written in 1950 by Mrs. John Raymond Carson and adopted by the General Assembly in 1966 reads: "I salute the flag of South Carolina and pledge to the Palmetto State love, loyalty and faith."

Authorized by resolution of the General Assembly in 1776, South Carolina's Great Seal comprises two elliptical areas connected by palmetto tree branches. On the left is a tall palmetto tree that represents the victors in the battle at Sullivan's Island. With it is a fallen, destroyed tree, that stands for the British fleet. Along with this appears the motto "Quis Separabit?" (Who Will Separate?), and it has twelve

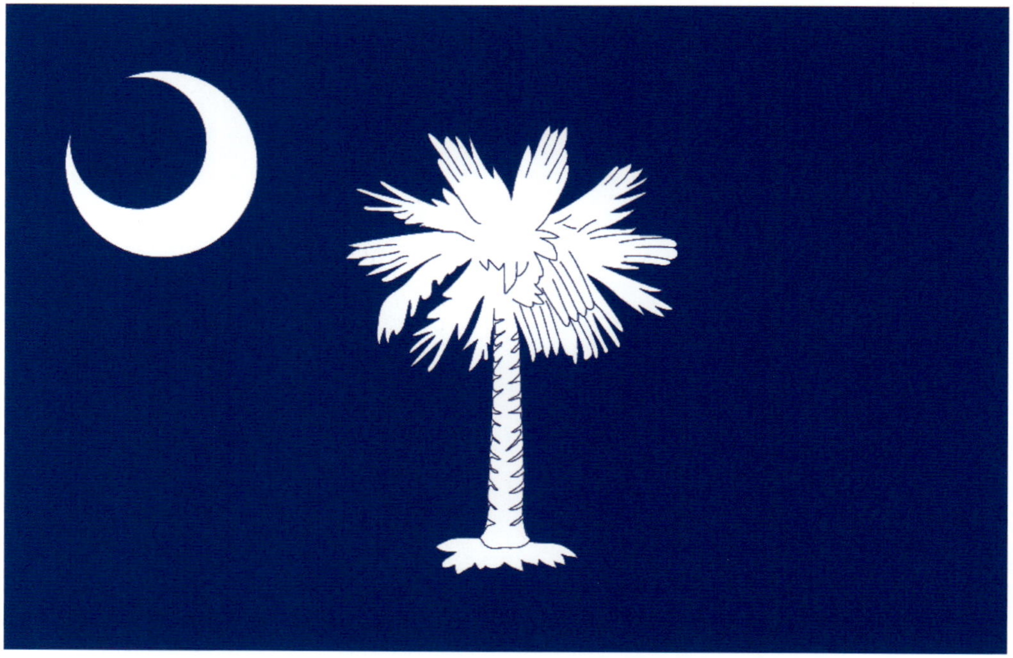

The State Flag of South Carolina

spears that represent the first states to join the Union. At the top "South Carolina" appears, and at the bottom one reads "Animis Opibusque Parati" (Prepared in Mind and Resources). The seal also shows a woman walking along the coast, amid weapons. The woman is Hope, and she holds a laurel branch. The sunrise is behind her, and at her feet we see "Spes," which identifies her as "Hope." The motto "Dum Spiro Spero" (While I Breathe, I Hope) is above her image.

The eighth coin released in the 50 State Quarters Program, the South Carolina quarter displays a palmetto tree, yellow jessamine, and the Carolina wren. On the back of the coin is an image of the state itself, the phrase "The Palmetto State," and a star that symbolizes Columbia. In 1998 the South Carolina Department of Parks, Recreation, and Tourism began to take quarter design suggestions. The governor, Jim Hodges, chose the winner. He felt that the palmetto stood for the strength of South

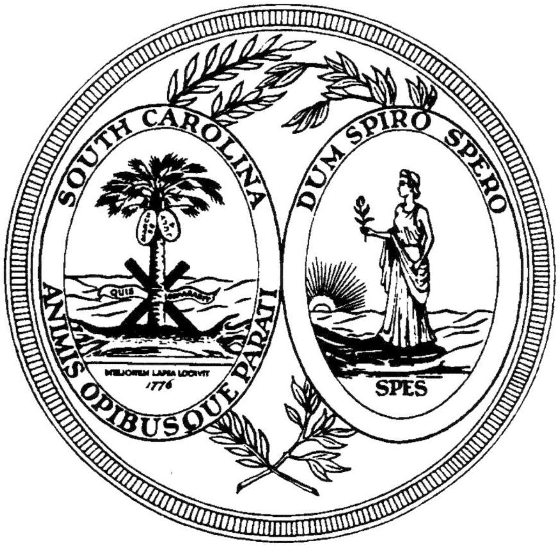

The Great Seal of South Carolina

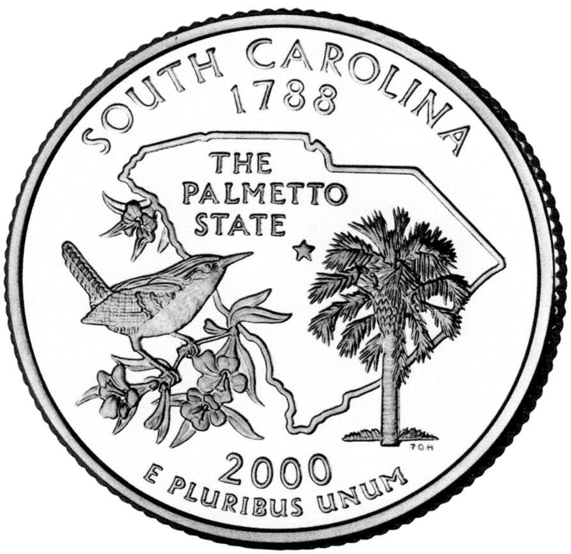

The South Carolina Quarter. United States Mint image.

Carolina; the Carolina wren, the state's hospitality; and the yellow jessamine, the state's natural beauty.

LITTLE MORE THAN A DECADE OR TWO AGO, it was rare to ever see South Carolina's state flag outside of an official setting. Today, the word palmetto can be found in the names of countless businesses, and South Carolina's flag and state emblem can be found on everything from flip-flops to crystal. One would be hard pressed to walk into any gift shop in South Carolina and not find the palmetto prominently featured on a wide range of items. The tree has become deeply embedded in South Carolina culture as a symbol exuding "Old South" hospitality and tradition and a defining a certain strength and independence that the state has been known for throughout its history.

Not only a popular cultural symbol of the state for commerce, the palmetto tree is featured in the logo for the University of South Carolina. In use since the founding of the university in 1801, the logo symbolizes the state's proud heritage. A graphic representation combines the images of a palmetto tree and the campus's Horseshoe area's gates. The gates stand for the openings in life provided by higher education, and the tree reflects stability and knowledge. The logo is often featured on many USC materials, merchandise, and signs.

The University of South Carolina Logo